GW00866451

This may well be one of the most info................,...........,
the most elegant website I've ever visited. – *Linda QM*

and a beautiful, well formed poop is nearly elegant......(: In fact
your website should be required reading in medical schools not to
mention vet education. Bravo! – *Helen*

Thank you so much for putting this valuable information out
on the web. I can't tell you how much I needed to have it all
spelled out for me. Even the best of vets can't spend the time to
go over all of the options and scenarios; so to have it all here at my
fingertips when I'm at another decision point with my cat is truly
appreciated. – *Heidi*

What an impressive and ingenious site! I have it bookmarked
for ready reference. – *Marilyn*

I never saw your site before ... it is amazing! Very informative. –
Leonor

Was just introduced to this amazing website. I'm shocked at
how much I don't know about the digestive system. I asked a friend
for suggestions and she said I must read this website first. – *Linda
H*

Thank you so much for your site! I am very grateful for all
your work to put together such useful information in an easily
accessible way. Our Amelio was born without use of his back legs
and some trouble with his digestion. We have really benefited from
your site. – *Judy*

This site is awesome! Thank you for creating it. – *Gwen*

What an amazing website! Your research and advice is spot on,
and I LOVE what you've done with simple black and white + the
animation is really clever. – *www.catfaeries.com:/*

Feline Constipation

"Cats require purity and simplicity." – SEM

Type to enter text
ISBN: 978-1-304-25239-5

Feline Constipation

Pat Erickson

This book is an adapted version of website
Feline Constipation ❖ Org

"Cats require purity and simplicity." – SEM

CONTENTS

🐾 Introduction

First, to ensure we are on the same page, here are several definitions and/or possible symptoms of constipation:

• infrequent (and frequently incomplete) bowel movements
• hard dry stools
• straining at stool*
• vomiting during or after pooping
• a change in frequency of bowel movements
• liquid stool from above leaking past impacted stool below, giving an appearance or impression of diarrhea
• with cats, out-of-box pooping may point to constipation
• visible blood on the stool
• any significant change in color or appearance

Note that straining to urinate could be confused with straining at stool. A cat who is unable to urinate is experiencing a medical emergency and must be seen by a vet immediately.

If the regular vet is not open, if it is a weekend or holiday, find the nearest veterinary emergency clinic.

"Cats require purity and simplicity." – SEM

Constipation is not only miserable for cats, it is unhealthy. Constipation can be the result of illness or disease and/or it can contribute to illness or disease. Constipation can be acute (temporary) or chronic (ongoing). A constipated cat can be helped.

The best treatment for a constipated cat is a human who understands how things work – how the digestive tract works, what poop is and is not, which remedies can help and which can harm or be ineffective. We need a foundation upon which to pin various facts and details, like that familiar childhood game of Pin The Tail On The Donkey. I hope to provide a serviceable donkey as well as some tails and that the tails hit the mark.

While I have tried to keep the writing as straightforward as possible without oversimplification, gut health and constipation can be a complex subject. The Glossary is included to help with unfamiliar terms. Illustrations enhance the text. Each topic offers highlighted points which are all gathered together in the Review section.

The general topic is divided into several subheadings intended to help you to better understand gut health and constipation. We usually focus on results or lack of results in the litter box; we put our focus on the end product. Since that is not where trouble starts, I encourage you to read the topics in order. If the situation in your house is tense, skip ahead to Acute Treatment and come back later when you're feeling calmer.

No one needs to pass a written test. Take your time, give yourself credit for any gain in understanding how things work. Confusion precedes learning so initial confusion is a good thing!

Most of what I have learned, I learned after our cat SEM died of Chronic Renal Failure in 2001. I surely wish I had known and understood more when SEM was alive and hope this information will help you to help your own cat.

This information is not a substitute for proper veterinary diagnosis and treatment.

 My intent is to inform. It is your responsibility to seek an accurate diagnosis and proper treatment for your cat from a trained professional.

Errors of omission or commission remain my own.

Pat Erickson

"Cats require purity and simplicity." – SEM

🐾 The First Lesson

Running from mouth to anus through the middle of ourselves and our cats, **the inside of the tube called the digestive tract is not inside the body** where vital organs such as the kidneys and the heart reside. The gut wall acts as a barrier between outside and inside.

If a cat swallowed a little marble, it would travel inside that tube, move on through the digestive tract as through a marble run, and eventually get pooped out. The marble would not get inside the body itself, it is too large to fit through the 'gateways' of the gut wall to get into the body, it would remain inside that tube and pass out the other end in the poop.

The bladder would never see that marble, the marble would not exit in the urine. **The bladder is inside the body and handles waste products from inside by dumping them into the urine. Poop is waste from the gut, outside the body itself.**

This inside/outside business is vital to understanding gut health and constipation so please take a few extra seconds to imagine a repeat marble run until the concept is clear.

Imagine that after that marble exits, instead of landing in the litter box it rolls back up along the cat's belly to the mouth. If that image is uncomfortable for you, feel free to imagine washing the marble first. When the marble reaches the mouth, it is back where it started. Imagine it being swallowed and traveling through the digestive tract again. Never once does it enter the inside of the body, never could it contact the internal organs, no matter how many times this exercise is repeated.

The lining of the digestive tract is an extension of the skin and the skin is an extension of the lining. Skin seamlessly shifts to lining right at the inner lipline, check in a mirror to remind yourself. Checking your own lips may be easier than checking those of your cat, cats being cats.

We tend to think of skin as a sort of wallpaper but the skin, including its gut wall extension, is the largest organ of the body. Skin is not paper thin, it is composed of various complex layers and performs active functions.

For the eater, the gut wall is the first line of defense between the outside world and the inside of the body.

Understanding that the inside of the gut is not inside the body is fundamental to understanding what follows, which is why it is the first lesson.

Swallowing food gets food into the digestive tract, into the gut, not into the body. Before food can be put to use in the body, it needs to be digested and then absorbed into the body.

"Cats require purity and simplicity." - SEM

The same is true for drinking water, swallowing puts water into the digestive tract, not into the body. Water does not require digestion but it does need to be absorbed before it can be put to use for its various purposes in the body.

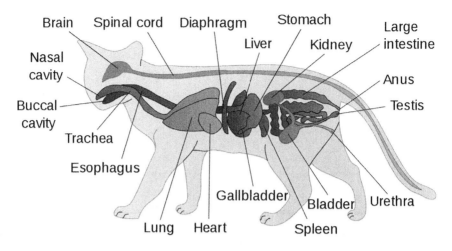

Brain Spinal cord Diaphragm Stomach
Nasal cavity Liver Kidney Large intestine
Buccal cavity Anus
Trachea Testis
Esophagus
Gallbladder Bladder Urethra
Lung Heart Spleen

http://commons.wikimedia.org/wiki/Media:Scheme_cat_anatomy-en.svg

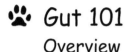 Gut 101
Overview

To understand what goes wrong and why, we first need to understand how things work. Understanding constipation requires understanding gut function.

The digestive tract starts at the mouth and ends at the anus with the esophagus, the stomach, the small intestine, and the large intestine in between, all hooked together in a long continuous complex tube. While it is easy enough to imagine the course as a marble run, no swallowed marbles allowed even though, as we learned in The First Lesson, inside that tube is not inside the body proper.

The digestive system includes organs that are actually inside the body but work closely with the digestive tract - the liver, the gall bladder and the pancreas. Not all those organs are pictured above and our focus is on the digestive tract, not on the internal digestive organs.

"Cats require purity and simplicity." – SEM

The inner lining of the entire digestive tract consists of mucous membrane. Mucous membranes secrete mucous from special glands which are particularly abundant in the gut. *Mucous* keeps passages moist and serves other purposes including playing a role in immune function. It also *makes the digestive tract self-lubricating.*

Like the walls of the bladder, blood vessels and other internal organs, *the gut wall is composed of smooth muscle cells whose action is involuntary*, that is, it is not under conscious control. Once a bite of food is swallowed, the gut's very own nervous system, the enteric nervous system or ENS, takes over control from the central nervous system.

A remarkable system, the enteric nervous system, governs the digestive tract. *The enteric nervous system is a huge affair; its cells make up a majority of the peripheral nervous system!* Older anatomy texts such as Gray's Anatomy make no mention of this vast system because its confirmation is so recent.

A division of the peripheral nervous system (PNS) as opposed to the central nervous system (CNS), the ENS can run on its own if need be. It is worth pausing to ponder this remarkable system. Here is what one pioneer researcher, Michael D. Gershon, MD, wrote eloquently about the ENS in his book, The Second Brain:

> *[The gut] is the only organ that contains an intrinsic nervous system that is able to mediate reflexes in the complete absence of input from the brain or spinal cord . . . There are more than a hundred million nerve cells in the human small intestine, a number roughly equal to the number of nerve cells in the spinal cord. Add on the nerve cells of the esophagus, stomach, and large intestine and you find that we have more nerve cells in our bowel than in our spine. We have more nerve cells in our gut than in the entire remainder of our peripheral nervous system. The enteric nervous system is also a vast chemical warehouse within which is represented every one of the classes of neurotransmitter found in the brain. Neurotransmitters are the words nerve cells use for communicating with one another and with the cells under their control.*
>
> Gershon, M. D. The Second Brain: XIII.
> HarperCollins Publishers, Inc., New York, NY.
> Quoted by kind permission of the author

Keep the general concept, if not the details, of the enteric nervous system in mind. It is sufficient to know that this vast network of nerves exists, dedicated to informing and supporting the gut. Attention to the health of the ENS plays a role in preventing constipation.

The gut wall also contains cells called Interstitial Cells of Cajal or ICCs. These specialized cells act as pacemakers for the rhythm of the gut wall's contractions, contractions whose timing varies from section to section. Research of ICCs is ongoing, science doesn't know everything about them yet, but we could think of them as dance choreographers.

The gut wall is more than a passive barrier between the lumen (the inside space of the intestinal tract) and the inside of the body; it is an active and dynamic organ.

Food

Food provides nourishment for the body to fuel, build, repair and maintain itself and all its parts. Food consists of proteins, fats, carbohydrates and fiber plus vitamins and minerals. And, of course, food contains water so nourishes and hydrates. Food (and water) has kept life going on Earth for millions of years. Food is life.

A quick note about the body's water content. Water is everywhere in the body, it is a given. Even when not specifically mentioned, we should imagine water as part of the equation, whether discussing food or digestion or absorption. Water is the major component of blood and of the interstitial fluid and other body fluids, the fluid outside the blood vessels.

The nourishment in food is locked up in complex molecules that, before digestion, are too large to get through the barrier of the gut wall into the blood stream and thus into the body. First food must be digested.

As we learned in The First Lesson, the inside of the gut is not the inside of the body, it is the inside of the gut. The gut is open to the outer world at both ends and the world is not a sterile place. Food is not always sterile, it certainly was not sterile when cats were on their own in the wild. Yet the actual inside of the body needs to be protected from bacteria. Stomach acid evolved about 350,000,000 years ago, in species who developed digestive tracts, in order to help protect the eater from incoming pathogens. Under normal circumstances, stomach acid kills incoming bacteria.

How to turn food into cat? We do not staple or sew a piece of chicken into a cat. First the chicken must be digested, broken down into the smallest elements, absorbed into the body, and there put to use for the cat's own purposes. It is not like ship-in-a-bottle, the cat does not recreate chicken after getting the small bits inside, she makes cat out of chicken.

Before food can nourish, it must be digested so it can be absorbed into the body.

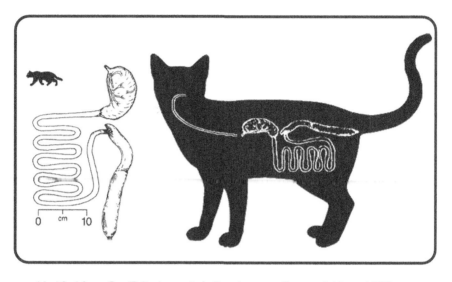

Modified from Cat (Felis domestica) digestive tract (Stevens & Hume 1995)
http://www.cnsweb.org/digestvertebrates/WWWEdStevensMammalCat.html
Reproduced by kind permission of Cambridge University Press,
32 Avenue of the Americas, New York, NY 10013-2473, USA

"Cats require purity and simplicity." – SEM

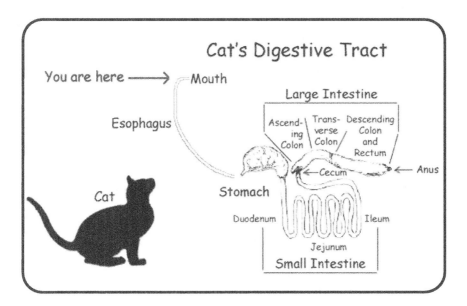

Mouth

A cat may or may not chew a bite of commercial cat food much before she swallows it. Saliva, a mixture of mucous, water, electrolytes and enzymes, has enzymes with antimicrobial properties which can protect against some food-borne bacteria. Cats on commercial diets do not tend to chew enough to make as much use of saliva as when cats were hunting for themselves. A mouse takes more gnawing and the section of mouse the cat is gnawing spends more time in contact with saliva.

Still saliva moistens and lubricates food and saliva contains buffers which can alter the pH of the mouth's contents and protect the esophagus. We often see a cat swallow several times in quick succession before vomiting. Stomach contents are highly acidic and the esophagus is not protected from contact with acid as the stomach is protected. When vomiting threatens, more saliva is produced, saliva to be swallowed to temporarily coat the esophagus against the acid bath soon to follow. We experience the same, our mouths 'water' and we swallow extra saliva before we vomit.

Saliva-coated food does not quite touch the walls of the esophagus, it is separated from direct contact by a thin coating of saliva.

The action of the teeth, tongue and mouth help to shape and prepare the food for swallowing, which is a surprisingly complex and delicately coordinated process. The pre-processing of food in the mouth, even kibble, prepares it for the trip ahead.

The cat swallows the bite and the food moves through the upper esophageal valve or sphincter in the back of the throat into the esophagus.

A note here about oral bacteria: Bacteria live in everyone's mouth and cats are no exception. Bacteria also need to eat, using their own enzymes to digest or ferment food. Oral bacteria do not ferment protein or fat, they ferment carbohydrates. There is often heated debate as to whether kibble does or does not clean teeth and which types of food contribute to dental decay in cats. Bacteria in organized groups form plaque, which then turns to tartar. Their fermentation byproducts are irritating to mouth tissue, especially to the gums if the bacteria manage to take up residence below the gumline. The gums response is to inflame which pulls them away from their tight fit against the teeth, leaving more space for tartar buildup. Bacteria have eons of practice at meeting their needs. They also need food to live and reproduce, just as the rest of us do.

Food that does not remain in the mouth is not available to ferment in the mouth.

The cat's jaw is wired for up-and-down movement only, no sideways movement, so their ability to retrieve stray food particles and residue is very limited. You can check this out yourself by trying to run your tongue around the outsides of your teeth without allowing your jaw to shift to the side.

Esophagus

Once in the esophagus, the swallowed food is inched down by peristalsis, a snakelike action of the esophageal wall that moves in one direction. Many people are surprised by the length of the esophagus. As the illustrations above depict, it runs from the back of the mouth down through the neck and chest and passes through the diaphragm before connecting with the stomach.

When the esophagus is empty, the walls collapse forming a closed space. They open and expand in response to swallowed foods and liquids.

The esophagus evolved in concert with water and food which not only move along well in response to peristalsis but make it easier for the esophagus to move them along because they are not unyielding like tablets and gelcaps. There's a reason we're told to swallow pills with a full glass of water. *For cats, all solid medications and supplements should be 'chased' with sufficient food or water to ensure they make the long journey successfully and do not become entrapped in the esophagus. Chasing liquid medications is also a nice courtesy to avoid potential irritation of the tender mucosa.*

When food or liquid reaches the end of the esophagus, the lower esophageal or cardiac valve opens to allow access into the stomach. Closing securely behind is important to prevent 'heartburn', so nothing from the stomach comes back up into the esophagus. The lining of the esophagus is not designed for exposure to stomach acid or for anything to linger long there.

Still sometimes stomach contents do come back up if a cat vomits. When vomiting is imminent, an excess of saliva is produced. The swallowed saliva temporarily protects the esophagus with a coating of buffered fluid so the esophagus is not burned by stomach acid. We humans do the same; we feel our mouths 'watering' before we vomit.

This is a good place to mention the difference between vomiting and regurgitation. Vomiting is the forceful ejection of acidic stomach contents. Regurgitation is a gentler release of non-acidic esophageal contents and the food retains the shape of the esophagus, looking like a sausage or even sometimes mistaken for poop.

Stomach

Once food is in the stomach, the work begins. The stomach environment is very acidic but the stomach wall is protected from contact with acid by a thick layer of mucous. The strong stomach musculature kneads and blends, with assistance from gastric rugae, folds of the stomach wall which boost action like the fins of a washing machine agitator, churning and kneading and smushing the food mixture into a smooth thick soup called chyme. This action is mechanical digestion which starts the breakdown process.

The rugae, those folds of the stomach wall, also allow the stomach to expand in response to a volume food. Although we think of the stomach as a digestive organ, which it is, it is mainly a storage organ which allows us to eat more at one time than without a stomach. Digestion can be accomplished without a stomach, the small intestine can do the job on its own. But if we were entirely dependent on the small intestine for digestion, we could eat only a very small amount at one time, we would have to eat almost continuously, and digestion would take longer without the stomach's mechanical digestion and predigestion of protein as we learn below. Holiday meals would be impossible and a cat in the wild would be unable to eat the whole mouse while opportunity is at hand, or paw as it were.

Without a stomach's acidic environment, all of us, cats and humans alike, would be more subject to food-borne illness and bacterial overgrowth.

Additional water can be requested from the body stores if there was insufficient water in the food, as well as more gastric acid to maintain a desirable pH. Although the gut wall acts as a barrier, permissible traffic can go both ways.

Stomach acid, in addition to killing incoming bacteria, 'denatures' protein; it unfolds the amino acid chains that make up protein for better access by pepsin. Pepsin is an enzyme synthesized by special glands in the stomach.

Denaturing protein is akin to chemical hair straightening since stomach acid relaxes the folds or curls just as hair straightener relaxes the hair. Hair is, after all, made of a special kind of protein called keratin.

Below is a representation of one protein in its folded state, on the left, and in its denatured state on the right. I have reversed the original image for this purpose. You can see how denaturing or unfolding gives enzymes better access to these otherwise complex protein structures. Hair, incidentally, is neither digestible nor fermentable by the cat or her gut bacteria.

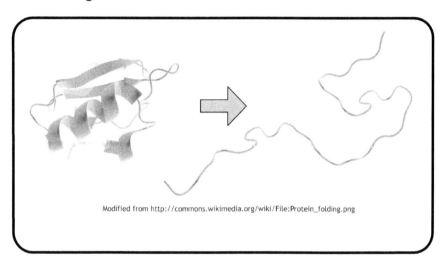

Modified from http://commons.wikimedia.org/wiki/File:Protein_folding.png

The action of enzymes on food is called chemical digestion or enzymatic hydrolysis. Enzymes break down larger molecules into smaller and smaller molecules. They break chemical bonds at various points along the way. Enzymes themselves are constructed of amino acids. The body makes the necessary enzymes, for digestion and metabolic processes.

Chemical (enzymatic) digestion of protein starts in the stomach with the aid of those special glands in the stomach which secrete pepsin. As a chain of amino acids, protein is not a string of beads and enzymes are not scissors but the image below illustrates that pepsin snips longer strings of amino acids into small units called peptides.

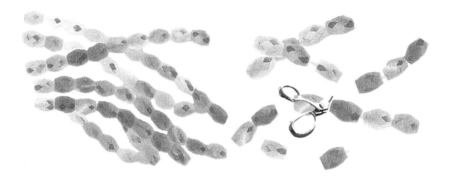

Pepsin does not alter the amino acids themselves, pepsin alters the length of the protein strands to prepare them for absorption into the body.

Protein digestion is completed in the small intestine. Carbohydrates and fats wait until the small intestine for their chemical digestion; in the stomach they are blended and smushed by mechanical digestion.

When the chyme is sufficiently liquified and blended into proper consistency, it is released bit by bit through the pyloric valve into the small intestine. Thanks to complex fluid dynamics and elegant design, larger bits requiring more work get tossed back by stomach action for further digestion. In the meantime, receptors in the duodenum, the first part of the small intestine following the stomach, detect what it is being received and what the body needs to receive which helps set the pace of the discharge from the stomach.

The stomach doesn't drain like a bathtub, its emptying is an orchestrated process, a process dependent on the chemical mix of the chyme and the needs of the body. If the body's need for nourishment is not immediate, the process can be slowed to keep pace. If the last meal was too long ago, the process can be stepped up. If the chyme has a high fat content, gastric emptying may be slowed to better control the upcoming absorption process.

"Cats require purity and simplicity." – SEM

😺 Gut 102
Recap

In Gut 101, we saw that the digestive tract is one long continuous tube running through the body from mouth to anus, and that the inside of that tube is outside of the body, with the gut wall separating the two. We followed food through the stomach and are set to enter the small intestine. Here again is our map:

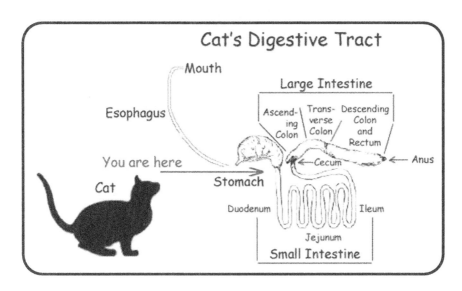

Small Intestine

A reminder that even when not specifically mentioned, we should imagine water as part of the discussion, as the major component of blood and of the interstitial fluid and other body fluids, the fluid outside the blood vessels.

The small intestine is the major digestion and absorption site and is divided into three sections - the duodenum, the jejunum, and the ileum. The jejunum is the longest section of the small intestine. The differences among these three sections involve some differences in internal responsibility and function but they would not be evident by looking from the outside. Disease of the small intestine tends to be defined as a whole, not necessarily specific to one of its parts.

As a tubular organ, the inner space of the small intestine is called the lumen. Lumen is not the term for the gut wall but for the space inside the gut.

The small intestine is long, about two and a half times the length of the cat on average. Not every cat is average and the individual length may vary. This length is cleverly arranged to fit in a smaller space. The 'map' above shows the small intestine as a folded affair in order to indicate relative length in relationship to the cat. For clarity, other illustrations may show the small intestine looking more like a string of sausage, as in the first illustration below.

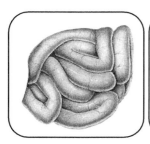  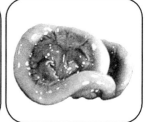

"Cats require purity and simplicity." - SEM

In fact **the small intestine is a creatively ruffled affair,** as we see more clearly in the second image, with the arrangement of the rufflings and riffles of the small intestine varying from individual to individual.

In the third, a photo of cat small intestine with the small intestine partially unruffled, we now see evidence of the mesentery, a membrane that anchors the small intestine to the back wall of the abdominal wall cavity. *The mesentery is an elegant evolutionary development, a membrane that not only anchors the small intestine yet still allows flexibility of the organ plus provides pick-up-and-delivery service for all those nutrients that are being released from the food.*

How is this design trick accomplished? The mesentery is created by an ingenious folding of the peritoneum. And what is the peritoneum? As skin covers the outside of the body, the peritoneum lines the inside of the abdominal cavity. We could compare the peritoneum to the inner lining of a storm coat, except it does not zip out. Instead it folds itself in remarkable ways during embryonic development, while the fetus is forming.

On the following page is an illustration of the mesentery which show the mesentery's physical connection to the small intestine along with the blood vessels which pick up and transport nutrients throughout the body after digestion in the gut. The mesentery is constructed of a double fold of the peritoneum which wraps around the small intestine and, just as the trailing edge of a ruffle is anchored to a neckline or a sleeve cuff, this mesenteric arrangement is anchored to the back wall of the abdominal cavity. The small intestine is secured yet able to give and stretch as chyme flows through its lumen.

This illustration shows only a small length of small intestine with its corresponding mesentery so a more complete understanding is presented later in this chapter. Here it is enough to know that the small intestine is not flopping around loose inside one's cat.

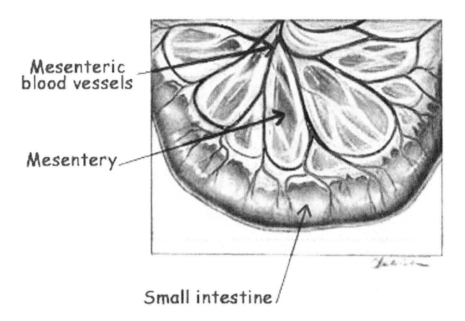

Mesenteric blood vessels

Mesentery

Small intestine

Immediately after the chyme enters the duodenum, the first part of the small intestine, *the acid from the stomach is neutralized by a buffer, a bicarbonate,* delivered from the pancreas via the pancreatic duct. Only the stomach is designed to handle its strong gastric acid, not the esophagus nor the small intestine.

Enzymes from the pancreas are delivered to the duodenum to digest carbohydrates, fats, and to complete the digestion of protein. Different enzymes are required to break down different substances, they are specialists. Cells in the villi of the gut wall also synthesize enzymes which assist with breakdown and absorption of various nutrients.

Bile also has neutralizing effects on the stomach acid. *Bile, synthesized by the liver and stored in the gall bladder, enters into the duodenum via the bile duct to emulsify edible fats present in the chyme, resulting in a milky mix called chyle.* The detergent action of bile breaks down larger fat molecules into smaller molecules and allows the fats to mix with watery lymph which gives greater access to the lipases, fat digesting enzymes from the pancreas. Mix emulsified fats with lymph in the gut and we have chyle. Bile itself does not become a part of the chyle that is later absorbed into the body.

Lymph fluid starts as interstitial fluid, the body's fluid outside the blood circulatory system and outside the cells, surrounding all the cells. Once interstitial fluid enters the lymph system, it is by definition lymph fluid and its composition changes as it flows along through its own circulatory system.

The neutralized chyme flows through the small intestine like a slow swirling river, propelled along by both peristalsis and segmentation. These are different but complementary actions which move chyme along (peristalsis) while simultaneously mixing it (segmentation). We can see why specialized cells such as the Interstitial Cells of Cajal, the ICCs, are needed to help coordinate all these movements. These two actions maximize the access of enzymes to their molecular targets and also maximize contact with the villi and absorption into the body. As we read above, the small intestine has a rich blood supply; blood vessels and the lymph system are the transport systems of the body, the pickup and delivery.

As the chyme swirls and flows through the jejunum, molecules of digested nutrients contact the villi and are absorbed via the mesentery into the blood system for distribution to all parts of the body where they are put to use.

In the last section of the small intestine, the ileum, Vitamin B12 from meat sources is absorbed.

Some bile salts are resorbed back into the body in the ileum for recycling. Remember that permissible traffic can go both ways through the gut wall barrier.

Other nutrients which were not absorbed in the jejunum get a last chance in the ileum where additional enzymes are provided by cells in the villi.

A common theme develops. *Digestion breaks bigger pieces into smaller and smaller pieces. Mechanical digestion uses physical means to break down big pieces, for greater surface area and better enzymatic access. Chemical digestion employs enzymes to snip into smaller molecules by breaking chemical bonds that hold compounds together.* Food needs to be broken down before it can cross the gut wall barrier into the blood stream.

That illustration above, of the mesentery, is a view from the outside, not inside the tube we call the gut or digestive tract, not in the lumen. Since the gut wall forms an active barrier between the lumen and the body, to regulate what crosses the barrier, how do those digested food molecules manage to get into the blood stream for transport inside the body? The food is digested but how does it get into the body to nourish the cat? Here is Nature's solution and once again folding is involved, this time of the inner lining of the small intestine into folds called plicae circulares.

On and between these folds are millions of tightly packed little fingerlike projections called villi, more so in the jejunum than in the duodenum. Villi increase surface area manyfold. If a human small intestine were unfolded to flatten all the villi and microvilli, it would cover more area than a football field!

The villi are in turn covered with microvilli. This greatly increased surface area and the richness of the blood supply allow more nutrients to be absorbed without the need to make the small intestine even longer. Folding is remarkably useful.

Not only do the villi and their microvilli expand the inner surface area of the small intestine, they also serve as loading docks and gateways.

If we were looking at a patch of villi with our naked eye, it would look as Henry Gray described it in his Gray's Anatomy, as having "a velvety appearance." That poetic description indicates just how thickly populated the wall of the intestine is with villi, like microfiber only more so. Another term for a surface covered with villi and microvilli, equally descriptive, is 'brush border'. *There may be 6,000 to 25,000 villi per square inch of intestinal wall, depending on the species whose intestine it is and the particular section of the intestine.* Think lush! The numbers per square inch decrease as we move downstream in the intestine and are thickest in the jejunum where most nutrient absorption takes place.

Here is a greatly magnified view which gives a hint of the microvilli covering the villi.

Gray's Anatomy, a text devoted to human anatomy, provides an illustration of cat intestinal villi including the mucosa and muscle layer of the wall. The villi may look tall in these graphics but they are only about 0.5 to 1 millimeter (mm) in length. A postage stamp is about 0.1 millimeter thick.

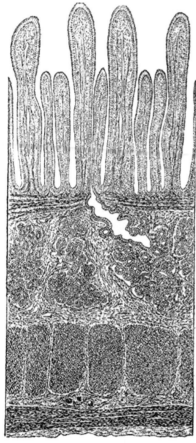

Villi

Intestinal glands

Muscularis mucosæ

Duodenal glands in submucosa

Circular muscular layer

Longitudinal muscular layer

Serous coat

Remember the villi carpet the lining of the small intestine, they are the lining of the small intestine, and all this folding greatly expands the effective surface area of the small intestine. Nature does a lot of folding.

FIG. 1058 – Section of duodenum of cat. (after Schäfer.) X 60.
Henry Gray (1825-1861). Anatomy of the Human Body. 1918.

That graphic gives us a hint of the complexities, a suggestion that the little villi have something going on under their surface.

Another of Gray's illustration, a cutaway, reveals more with evidence of the plumbing of the individual villi, their blood

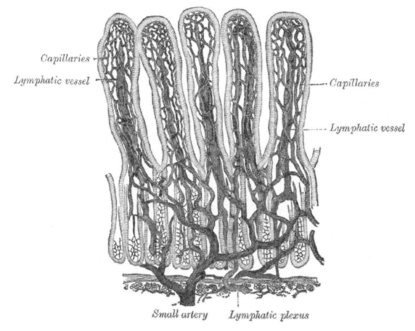

FIG. 1061 –Villi of small intestine, showiong bloodvessels and lymphatic vessels. (Cadiat.)Henry Gray (1825-1861).Anatomy of the Human Body. 1918.

and lymphatic vessels.
This is a good place to take a break and discuss circulatory systems before we return to the villi.

Just as the theme in digestion is to break big bits into smaller and smaller bits, a circulatory system has a similar theme, working from big through little, littler and littlest, down to the microcirculation level, and circulating back up through small to big again. Here is a

representation of an arrangement of a familiar circulatory system in one direction.

Turn the image upside down, mirror it, and what do we have?

Once Nature has a good system, it is used and reused and used yet again under a variety of circumstances. *A circulatory system functions as a pick-up-and-delivery system; the system can pick up, transport, and deliver useful and necessary goods or pick up, transport, and dump the waste.* Humans use similar graduated systems to deliver water

"Cats require purity and simplicity." – SEM

and electricity to dwellings and to remove waste.
The smallest blood vessels are not built to withstand the initial pressure of a heartbeat sending blood coursing through the arteries so blood pressure in the little capillaries is much less than blood pressure in the major arteries.

Capillaries connect the smallest arteries, the arterioles, which carry oxygenated blood away from the heart, to venules, the smallest veins, which carry blood back to the heart for reoxygenation. Capillaries also facilitate absorption into lymph vessels. The walls of the microscopic capillaries are only one cell layer thick, an important feature since capillaries are where the action is, where exchanges are made. *Capillaries are the key to*

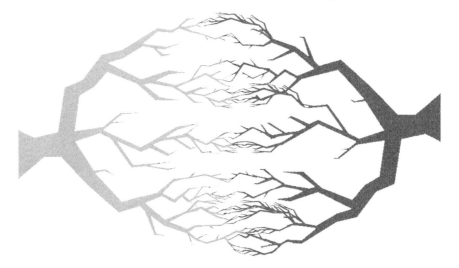

absorption of nutrients into the circulatory systems.
Above we have a representation of two networks intersecting, meant to illustrate connections between the arteries and the veins. Imagine capillaries at all the points where those two touch. If you have trouble imagining capillaries, think of your household wiring system which is hidden behind the walls but appears periodically at outlets

and switches and sockets, where you can access and interact with the electricity.

Now back to the villi. As we saw in Gray's illustration above, arteriols (the tiniest arteries) and venules (the tiniest veins) meet in each villi. But just like a household which has electrical wiring, plumbing and waste disposal, there are other systems in the body that need to be incorporated. In the case of the villi, we need to incorporate the lymph system and also take into account the enteric nervous system.

Here is a graphic of a single villus for further insight into its inner workings. Each part of the structure has an important and active function. Remember there are millions of these little villi and each villi is 'wired' into the body's blood circulatory system.

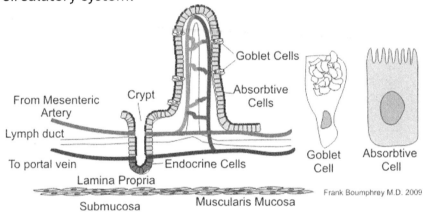

As we see, the outer surface of the villi consists of absorptive cells interspersed with goblet cells. **Goblet cells emit mucin which in contact with water forms mucous.** Mucin is composed of glycosylated proteins which dissolve in contact with water to form a gel. In the body, mucous lubricates and protects mucous membrane and plays a role in immune function. Each villi, therefore, helps to keep the small intestine lubricated and actively protects from infection and contamination.

The villi also synthesize enzymes which further break down nutrients until they are small enough to be absorbed by the absorptive cells of the villi. Absorptive cells, as their name implies, absorb or take in nutrients from the nutrient-rich chyme.

Nutrients are absorbed from the fluid environment of the lumen into the internal fluid environment of the villi where they are picked up by the villi's blood or lymph capillaries and thus into their respective circulatory systems.

Absorption is not a single process but different strategies depending on what is to be absorbed. There are several possibilities or a combination of strategies.

• Active Transport – requires energy plus, usually, a specific carrier molecule to achieve the transfer

• Passive Diffusion – molecules moving from a region of higher concentration to a region of lower concentration to equalize the concentration

• Passive Absorption – osmosis, a selective diffusion process

• Facilitated Diffusion – requires a carrier but not usually energy; the 'gate' in the membrane may need to change shape to accommodate

• Endocytosis (Pinocytosis or Phagocytosis) – cellular ingestion of nutrients by engulfing the molecule, pinocytosis for small molecules, phagocytosis for larger molecules.

Most essential nutrients are actively transported, with the exception of minerals which use passive diffusion and may require a carrier molecule but do not require an energy source to make the transition.

• Small molecules such as electrolytes, water, small sugars and other water solubles are absorbed by passive diffusion or passive absorption.

• Amino acids require both energy and a carrier to make the leap so they are actively transported.

• Fat is absorbed by endocytosis.

The energy needed to power absorption, when energy is required, is provided by a chemical called adenosine triphosphate (ATP) which is produced in the body's cells by their mitochondria. Mitochondria are little power generators in every cell and there are many in each cell. The energy the mitochondria need to synthesize ATP is provided by food, sparked by the oxygen breathed in and transported around the body by the red blood cells and their iron component.

If you would like to see animations of the absorption processes, there is a good selection here: www.nutrition.jbpub.com/resources/animations.cfm?id#

Opposite is a more magnified view inside the tips of those villi.

In the second image opposite, thanks again to Henry Gray, we have a cross section of a single villus to better visualize the workings of this bustling community.

When we view these graphics, we need to imagine interstitial fluid bathing all the cells.

"Cats require purity and simplicity." – SEM

Lymph Capillaries in the Tissue Spaces

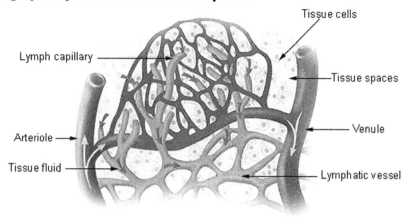

http://commons.wikimedia.org/wiki/File:Illu lymph capillary.jpg

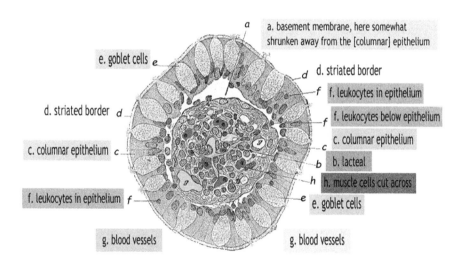

a. basement membrane, here somewhat shrunken away from the [columnar] epithelium

d. striated border

f. leukocytes in epithelium

f. leukocytes below epithelium

c. columnar epithelium

b. lacteal

h. muscle cells cut across

e. goblet cells

g. blood vessels

e. goblet cells

d. striated border

c. columnar epithelium

f. leukocytes in epithelium

g. blood vessels

FIG. 1060 – Transverse section of a villus, from the human intestine.
(v. .Ebner.) X 350.
Henry Gray (1825-1861). Anatomy of the Human Body. 1918.

Do you see those goblet cells emitting mucin? And do you see all those leukocytes, both in the epithelium (villi 'skin') and below the epithelium (inside the villi)? *Leukocytes are white blood cells and the villi are well stocked, especially with phagocytes like neutrophils and monocytes who attack potential invaders and gobble up debris.* If you have not seen this old video of a neutrophil chasing a bacterium, it is definitely worth watching and will, I think, alter your perception of white blood cells significantly. www.biochemweb.org/neutrophil.shtml

Finally we have the illustration below to bring the various concepts together.

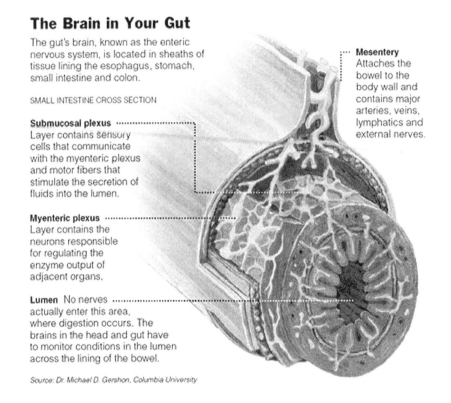

The Brain in Your Gut

The gut's brain, known as the enteric nervous system, is located in sheaths of tissue lining the esophagus, stomach, small intestine and colon.

SMALL INTESTINE CROSS SECTION

Submucosal plexus
Layer contains sensory cells that communicate with the myenteric plexus and motor fibers that stimulate the secretion of fluids into the lumen.

Myenteric plexus
Layer contains the neurons responsible for regulating the enzyme output of adjacent organs.

Lumen No nerves actually enter this area, where digestion occurs. The brains in the head and gut have to monitor conditions in the lumen across the lining of the bowel.

Mesentery
Attaches the bowel to the body wall and contains major arteries, veins, lymphatics and external nerves.

Source: Dr. Michael D. Gershon, Columbia University

There is the mesentery, the fold of the peritoneum which supports and anchors the small intestine. We see the enteric nervous system and the various layers of the structure, we clearly see the villi carpeting the interior.

That graphic points to an especially important aspect of the enteric nervous system – *communication between the ENS and the gut occurs across the lining of the gut without the ENS physically entering the lumen*. This communication utilizes neurotransmitters, particularly serotonin, in addition to physical pressure registered by the ENS. A majority of the body's serotonin is produced in the gut, serotonin which along with other neurotransmitters signals not only the ENS but also keeps the brain informed of the gut's doings. Remember that the lumen is the space in the intestines, the channel where the chyme flows.

No one needs to pass a test on all that material above. Some readers will be interested in the details, others will not. The main message is that this is a complex environment, not a simple tube, and a very important factor in the life and health of a cat.

The health of the cat depends on the health of the villi who themselves depend on good nutrition and nonexposure to toxic substances. Villi also require the physical passage of food in a use-it-or-start-to-lose-it response. In a cat (or a human or any species with small intestinal villi) who is not eating, the villi shrink. They can grow again, they can recover, but in the meantime health is at risk because both the gut barrier function and the ability to absorb nutrients are compromised.

Maintained by new cells migrating from the bottom up to their tips, in a continuous process, the old cells at the tips of the villi die and fall into the lumen where they are digested and anything reuseable is recycled, the rest passing out in the poop. Think of that cellular migration as a bucket brigade. The migration of cells depends on nutrition and the physical passage of food and will slow surprisingly quickly if meals are missed or a cat is not eating, as though not only is there no water for the bucket brigade but the buckets are missing.

The villi are also subject to damage by toxic substances, intestinal parasites, food allergies, food poisoning and anything that limits or cut off the blood flow or oxygenation to an area. Fortunately the fast cellular turnover in the villi means the gut wall has great healing capability when negatives are eliminated and a healthful diet is served and eaten regularly. Regularly for a cat means small frequent meals.

One of the important aspects of **the small intestine** is that it **evolved to transport liquidy contents, not solid objects**. The chyme delivered into the small intestine from the stomach is liquidy, not solid. Despite the marble run analogy in The First Lesson, solid objects do not flow along well. They are stiff and unyielding and the small intestine consists of many twists and turns. Trying to inch too large a solid object along that path is like trying to get a hefty piece of furniture around a tight corner or wrestled down a narrow hallway. The

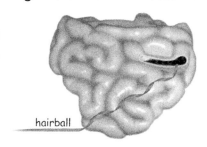

hairball

small intestine is flexible and expandable and it works hard at its job but still, it was designed for chyme, not hefty solid objects **such as formed hairballs** which might manage to escape the stomach downwards rather than get vomited up and out.

A linear foreign object, such as a string, is particularly risky because as it moves along, its length may occupy more than one turn of the small intestine and could cinch several sections together in a stranglehold, cutting off the blood supply to the area.

Bit by bit, as chyme reaches the end of the small intestine, it is released into the large intestine through the ileocecal valve, the sphincter or gate between the small and large intestines. By then, most everything which counts as a nutrient for the cat has been absorbed upstream and what's left, besides water, are the parts of the diet which can't be digested. These remainders are called dietary fiber and play a feature role in the large intestine.

We leave digestion and absorption at this point since our focus is in the gut, not inside the body. Readers interested in internal metabolism can find a remarkable amount of information on the web, in books stores and in the public library.

Large Intestine

Like the small intestine, the large intestine is anchored by its own mesentery which is called the mesocolon.

The first part of the large intestine is called the cecum. In cats, this section is very small in comparison to most other species and its function in cats is presently unknown.

The large intestine or colon wraps around the coiled-up small intestine. In humans, the ascending colon runs up the right side of the lower abdomen, the transverse colon travels across the abdomen, and the descending colon travels down the left side of the body where it turns a corner into the middle of the body and descends to the anus. There are many graphics illustrating this on the web.

In the cat, the arrangement is similar except a cat is much narrower across the midriff than a human. A cat's ascending colon is short in comparison and the transverse colon is also proportionally short. The descending colon runs horizontal because cats walk on all fours, but it is still called the descending colon as it descends to the anus. There is no last corner to turn. Positioned under the spine, the descending colon runs straight to the anus below the tail of the cat.

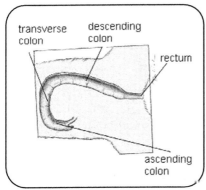
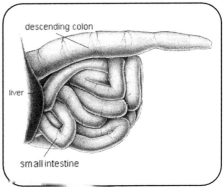

When the chyme reaches the large intestine or colon, electrolytes and excess water begin to be drawn off from the soupy chyme and resorbed into the body. *The large bowel makes poop out of soup!* If water and electrolytes weren't reclaimed, we'd all be dehydrated by constant diarrhea.

The large intestine or bowel is also where fermentable dietary fiber in the chyme is fermented by the trillions of gut bacteria who live in the bowel. These and other processes, discussed in the next chapters, result in what we call feces or stool or poop.

Formed poop is stored until time to move the bowels. *Pressure from the poop, moving into the rectum and pressing from the inside out on the nervous system of the bowel, the enteric nervous system, signals the bowel when it is time to move.* At this point in the process the signals from the enteric nervous system coordinate with nerve cells in the corresponding section of the spinal cord, of the central nervous system, to ensure that the spine cooperates in the best position for the poop to exit successfully. The proper squatting position facilitates pooping. Cats who have arthritis or who have suffered an injury to that area may experience constipation if the ENS and CNS are not able to coordinate at that juncture.

As stool moves from the rectum through the anal canal, the inner and outer anal sphincters relax and the canal shortens, effectively pulling this little 'storm porch' up and over the exiting stool as the rectal muscle exerts peristaltic contractions in response to the stool. The inner sphincter consists of smooth muscle without voluntary control but the outer sphincter is striated muscle and under voluntary control. And there it is, poop in the litter box!

Please do not skip over the next sections. It is important to understand the function of water and fiber in the whole process, and what poop is and is not, so that constipation can be treated and prevented as effectively as possible. It is especially important to read about the gut bacteria and their role in bowel health. The best treatment for a constipated cat is a caring human who has a general understanding of gut workings.

 Water

Water's role in constipation or lack of constipation is so frequently misunderstood that its relationship to constipation merits a chapter of its own.

The body needs to be properly hydrated for everything to work well. A dehydrated cat can also have a dehydrated stool. But a well-hydrated cat can still be constipated!

The problem of constipation is not necessarily lack of water in the cat, it is lack of water retention in the stool.

Water retained in the stool is what makes the difference between a softer stool and a harder stool. Proper treatment to prevent constipation involves increasing the water retention capacity of the stool.

Increasing the water retention capacity of the stool does not mean adding water to the cat unless the cat is dehydrated. If, without increasing the capacity of the stool to retain water, extra water is added to an adequately hydrated but constipated cat, that extra water will take the other exit and appear as urine in the litter box, it will not affect the poop.

What helps retain water in the stool?

Increasing water retention of the stool means improving the diet to improve the stool, making the changes necessary to ensure that happens. It may also involve the use of medication in a constipated cat. This is not a simple equation of 'add water' but involves understanding a bit of biochemistry. And that biochemistry involves the next chapter . . .

🐾 Gut Bacteria and Fiber

As mentioned in Gut 101, billions if not trillions of gut bacteria live in the cat's bowel. There are more bacteria there than there are cells in the body, several hundred different species of bacteria in uncountable numbers. The mix of bacterial populations in the host species differs somewhat so the mix in a cat will differ from that in a dog or a human but the principles are the same.

Gut bacteria live on dietary fiber, by definition the leftovers from food digestion, what was not digested and absorbed into the cat herself upstream in the gut. The bacteria also make use of shed gut wall cells. Due to heavy use, the gut wall is built to shed and renew its cells faster than other parts of the body, to maintain its integrity when properly nourished.

Food feeds the cat. Fiber feeds the gut bacteria.

The populations of gut bacteria living in the bowel qualify as an organ, as an organized functional unit dedicated to specific purposes, and this is the most metabolically active organ in the body. Not only do gut bacteria metabolize components of dietary fiber but they stimulate and 'train' the immune system, occupy territory to prevent foreign invaders from setting up housekeeping, synthesize vitamins, and play a key role in preventing constipation since their work factors in the creation of normal stools.

Important research about the role of fiber in the diet of the cat continues:

> *Although macronutrients (protein, fat, carbohydrates) and micronutrients (vitamins, minerals) are of obvious importance in maintaining the health of the GIT [gastro-intestinal tract – the gut], feeding diets with readily absorbed nutrients effectively "starves" the colon. This leads to disturbances of GIT characteristics and can have a detrimental impact on health. Diets without fiber reduce mucosal barrier functions and increase the risk of bacterial translocation and septicemia. These findings demonstrate that though fiber does not directly provide energy or nutrients, it can be considered an "essential" component of diets, and this includes diets for dogs and cats. When formulating diets there is a need to consider that they must provide nutrients for the host as well as for the bacteria resident in the GIT.*
>
> Buddington R. K., Buddington, K. K., Sunvold G. D. The Use of Fermentable Fibers to Manage the Gastrointestinal Tract. Recent Advances in Canine and Feline Nutrition 2000:169 Orange Frazer Press Wilmington, OH.

What does all that mean? It means that even though dietary fiber does not feed the cat herself, fiber is nonetheless essential for the health of the gut and therefore the health of the cat. There needs to be something in the diet that is not digestible and is not absorbable, that flows on to the gut bacteria waiting in the large intestine (aka the large bowel).

The phrase 'mucosal barrier functions' describes the necessary integrity of the gut wall, keeping it healthy and strong so what is being digested in the gut stays in the gut until it is ready to be absorbed into the body and so what does not belong stays out of the body and passes on out in the poop. The gut wall keeps gut bacteria in their place. We want those bacteria working in the bowel, outside the body itself, not invading or translocating into the body to cause septicemia, a toxic bacterial systemic infection.

Why do we care? Aren't bacteria bad news? Not necessarily. We live in the real world and the real world is not a sterile place, nor can we render ourselves sterile no matter how much we wash, no matter how many antiseptic products we use. We are all colonized starting at birth with trillions of bacteria on the outsides of ourselves and, as we learned, the gut is technically outside the body. Rather than try to keep bacteria away, alliances and truces were developed eons ago so that under normal circumstances, peace exists. Our familiar bacteria, those that live all over the skin and inside the gut help fend off and control less beneficial bacteria and other microscopic organisms. Our own bacteria depend on the host, in this case the cat, for their sustenance and, in turn, provide benefit to the cat. But rather than trust the alliances completely, the gut wall

"Cats require purity and simplicity." - SEM

actively works to keep bacteria in their work place and not invade the body and well kept bacteria contribute to maintaining the gut wall. This activity is the mucosal barrier function and proper fiber choices in the cat's diet help keep the desirable gut bacteria well fed and content in their assigned place so they continue to fulfill their end of the bargain, as we see below. A healthy gut wall performs good traffic control.

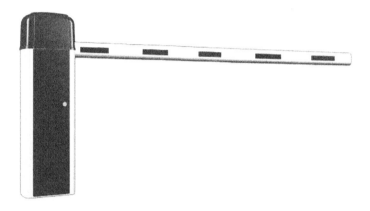

Food feeds the cat. Fiber feeds the gut bacteria. And the gut bacteria play an important role in helping to prevent constipation.

Since the gut wall barrier forms a significant part of the immune system, the gut bacteria are key players in maintaining healthy immunity as well.

Fiber is the parts of foods that cannot be digested or absorbed and what we call dietary fiber comes from plant material. Fiber can be insoluble (does not dissolve in water) or soluble (does dissolve). Fiber can be fermentable or nonfermentable. Fermentable means there are gut bacteria present in the crowd who can utilize or 'eat' or ferment that fiber source. A particular fiber is not fermentable unless someone is around to ferment it.

Insoluble fiber is considerably less fermentable than soluble fiber; it mainly acts as bulk to increase stool volume since it holds water like a sponge without dissolving in that water.

Soluble fiber is more fermentable, to varying degrees depending on which bacterial species are present to perform the job. *Few fiber sources and choices are all one or all the other, they are a mix of soluble and insoluble in varying percentages.* So a single fiber source can provide both bulk, with its water holding capacity, and provide food for the gut bacteria, who also influence the water retained in the stool and whose sheer numbers contribute to stool volume.

There are beneficial bacteria and pathogenic bacteria in the bowel as there are everywhere. A proper choice of fermentable fiber preferentially feeds the good guys and keeps their numbers higher. The good bacteria are those who provide benefit to the host, in this case the cat. The byproducts of the undesirable or pathogenic gut bacteria are irritating and toxic to the gut wall and the enteric nervous system.

If beneficial bacterial numbers are reduced by antibiotics or by lack of species-appropriate fermentable fiber and the less desirable bacteria flourish because their competition is reduced, a cat may experience bowel problems. Longer term, damage to the gut wall and the enteric nervous system could result.

Fiber is not visible, it is not like the strings on celery. In the human diet, a banana is rich in fiber even though its flesh is smooth. Fiber consists of certain nondigestible and nonabsorbable complex sugars present mainly in plant material, sugar complexes which digestive enzymes cannot digest (split apart), leaving them too large to be absorbed

upstream. Fiber is present in plants and in small amounts in whole prey such as mice. A cat consuming a whole mouse in the wild eats all of the prey plus the contents of the prey's digestive tract which include plant material. Cats tend to get most of their plant material indirectly. The prey eats the plants, the cat eats the prey.

A side note here about cats and plant material. Plants are unable to run away from danger or protect themselves by socking someone in the nose. Plants depend on physical protection such as a thick shell or rind, and/or chemical warfare. Plants are remarkable chemical factories, even our familiar veggies. All of those chemicals need to be properly metabolized by the eater to be safe for the eater, to avoid harm to the digestive system. Humans, as omnivores who eat a wide variety of foods, evolved with liver enzymes that can detoxify many plants chemicals. So did most of the cat's prey species like the mouse. But our carnivorous cats did not, they lack certain liver detoxification pathways that we take for granted. Since cats ate very little plant material directly, instead running most of their plant material through their prey first and then eating the prey, we need to make appropriate plant fiber choices for cats.

Because many of us think of the body in terms of mechanical function, we often think of fiber only as a bulking agent, bulking up the stool by holding water like a sponge to make the stool softer. I hope this chapter expands the understanding of fiber. Water, as we learned, is what makes the difference between a softer stool and a harder stool but bulking fiber is not the only way to achieve that end and not a desirable approach if it starves the gut bacteria.

The natural diet of cats does not contain much bulk; a cat's digestive tract is not designed for large bulky stools such as that of a herbivore. A normal stool for a cat is smallish in diameter and firmish but not rock hard. As a carnivore, a cat naturally produces a segmented stool, not pellets or patties.

The stool should be soft enough to mold when passing through the anus which is slightly smaller than the expanded rectum. But the stool should be firm enough to respond well to pressure from the gut wall when pushing the stool out. Poop that is too soft is like pushing a chain and may require extra effort. It also does not properly stimulate the anal glands of a cat which can lead to anal gland impaction.

A particular fiber in the diet is fermentable if there is a bacterial species present in the bowel population who is able to ferment it. Different species of bacteria ferment different fibers, just as different mammal or bird species eat different diets. Of course there is also overlap, just as the species of humans and cats alike eat turkey.

Food feeds the cat. Fiber feeds the gut bacteria. And the gut bacteria play an important role in helping to prevent constipation as well as maintaining the health and integrity of the gut wall.

Bacteria obviously digest their food sources outside their bodies, they lack an internalized gut. Bacteria 'digest' or ferment the dietary fiber they can make use of, using enzymes just as we do to split large molecules into smaller molecules, and in this process they produce short-chain fatty acids (SCFAs) which provide various benefits to the host (the cat).

One type of SCFA, butyrate (butyric acid), is the chief fuel for the cells of the gut wall. That fuel is important because the cells of the gut wall have a high turnover rate, they are renewed about every three days. All this cell renewal requires energy. As the barrier between the outside world and the inside of the body, it is essential that the intestinal wall has the fuel necessary to replace shed gut wall cells with new ones, to remain in good repair. The gut wall sees a lot of activity.

Another SCFA produced by gut bacteria is acetate (acetic acid) which plays an important role in liver fatty acid metabolism. Remember, although the inside of the digestive tract is outside of the body, the digestive system includes the liver as well as the gall bladder and pancreas so it should not surprise us that something produced by the gut bacteria in the large bowel could provide benefit to the liver.

There are other SCFAs produced by the gut bacteria which are important and which are under research so we will all know more in the future. What we know to date is that SCFAs are important and cats can only benefit as we learn more.

In addition, and this is especially important for a constipated cat, *the SCFAs produced by the beneficial gut bacteria help maintain the pH of the stool in the slightly acidic range which helps to retain water in the stool. Water retention in the stool is a function of chemistry.*

That means that simply adding water to the cat may not do the job.

This slightly acidic range also discourages pathogenic bacteria from setting up housekeeping and reproducing. Keeping the beneficial bacteria populations high means they can convert the nitrogenous (protein) waste products into themselves, into more friendly bacterial bodies made of protein, which prevents these more toxic protein waste products from harming the gut wall, turns lead into gold as it were. Harm to the gut wall can result in a higher cellular turnover rate, as the body struggles to heal, which then means even more nitrogenous waste products for pathogenic bacteria, a vicious circle. The more beneficial gut bacterial numbers, the more of their beneficial byproducts produced.

Gut bacteria also produce some B vitamins and Vitamin K. It is not clear yet whether those B and K vitamins are absorbed or whether they only benefit locally in the bowel.

Properly fed to keep their numbers higher, beneficial bacteria reduce the amount of physical space left for pathogenic bacteria. The beneficial bacteria who live directly on the gut wall actively work to protect their turf from invaders with ill intent.

This is a remarkable arrangement. The bacteria have a home and the host receives a multitude of benefits.

Please note that SFCAs, short-chain fatty acids, are not the same as essential fatty acids (EFAs) which most of us recognize as Omega 3s in salmon and other cold-water fish. The EFAs, the essential fatty acids DHA and EPA, are dietary components which the cat herself can digest and absorb.

The SFCAs are chemical byproducts the gut bacteria produce which benefit the digestive system and the poop.

Fermentable fiber in the diet is essential, not fiber just for 'bulk' in the stool as we are used to thinking, but fiber as food for the gut bacteria to keep the bowel healthy. Half or more of the dry matter weight of poop consists of gut bacteria, which leads us into the next chapter ...

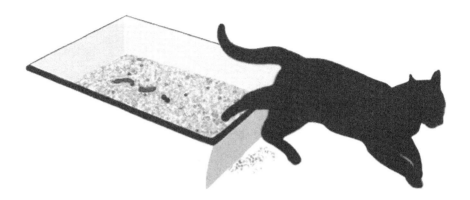

🐾 Poop

Poop also merits its own chapter. Not only do we celebrate cat poop in the litter box at home but in various online groups we celebrate cat poop the world around! Everyone feels a general sense of relief when a constipated cat manages to poop.

Poop is not leftover food. By definition, food is what feeds the cat herself and food, by definition is digestible and absorbable. The components of the diet that are not digestible are considered dietary fiber and move on into the bowel to become incorporated into the stool. That would include bound phosphorus if the cat is on a phosphorus binder.

Half or more of the dry weight of stool can be gut bacteria, zillions of them. They belong there. The remainder of the stool consists of short-chain fatty acids (SCFAs, the fermentation byproducts of the gut bacteria), some bile salts/acids that were not recirculated, shed gut wall cells from that high cellular turnover, mucous from the gut wall (sometimes visible), and anything from the diet that was nondigestible/nonabsorbable/nonfermentable.

The stool also contains bilirubin which comes from spent red blood cells, cells that have outlived their life span. Bilirubin is excreted in the bile. Bile is a greenish color and bilirubin has a yellowish hue. The gut bacteria change the yellow of bilirubin to the characteristic brown color of feces. We notice the yellow of bilirubin when the stool passes too quickly for bacterial action to change yellow to brown.

Mucous merits an additional word. Mucous is not digestible so even excessive swallowed mucous from an upper respiratory condition might conceivably be recognized in/on the stool. Mucous membrane lines the entire digestive tract, including the large intestine, membrane constantly producing mucous to one extent or another. So poop always contains mucous and is coated in mucous. Mucous membrane lines the upper respiratory tract, too, also constantly producing mucous to protect and lubricate itself, trap incoming foreign particles, and act as the frontline in immune function. Mucous from the upper respiratory tract continuously flows down the throat unnoticed and is swallowed, by ourselves and cats and dogs and other creatures with noses. Mucous is normal, chronic excessive production is not. We notice when production is excessive but do not tend to notice normal production.

While mucous is not digestible, it is fermentable to some extent. However, since the entire bowel is lined with mucous membrane which is constantly on the job, the poop is in contact with mucous right up to the moment it is expelled.

Of course poop contains water - water retained in the stool after the excess water from the soupy chyme upstream has been reclaimed back into the body itself.

Here is a recap of the main components of poop:

- Water
- Gut bacteria, 50% to 60% of the dry weight matter of normal poop
- Short Chain Fatty Acids (SCFAs) produced by the gut bacteria
- Bile salts that weren't recirculated
- Unabsorbed and/or recirculating electrolytes
- Shed gut wall cells as new cells take their places
- Mucous (perhaps visible mucous at times)
- Fiber that couldn't be fermented by the gut bacteria
- Anything swallowed that was not digestible or absorbable

The more water retained in the poop, the softer the poop. The less water, the harder the poop. More water means more volume which gives a clearer signal to the bowel muscle to move, a clearer invitation to dance. But not so much water that the stool is too soft. Soft stool can be equally hard to move out, like dancing with a rag doll.

As a carnivore, a cat naturally produces a firmish cylindrical segmented stool that may be tapered on one or both ends. The segments may separate on their drop into the litter box or from burial attempts. The drier the stool, the more likely the segments will separate or be separated and the smaller each segment may be.

The SCFAs which properly fed gut bacteria produce lower the pH of the bowel environment which in turn influences the amount of water the stool retains. A slightly acidic environment is necessary to retain sufficient water in the stool.

In cats, a stool that is too soft may not stimulate the anal glands sufficiently as the poop passes through the anus. That stimulation requires a firmer stool. If the anal glands are not regularly stimulated to discharge their contents, they can become impacted which can cause or worsen constipation. Anal gland impaction is painful for the cat and, left unattended, can result in infection and even rupture of the anal glands.

Any treatment for constipation, including laxatives and enemas, addresses the water retained in the poop and/ or present in the large bowel one way or another.

❁ What Goes Wrong?

Chronic conditions create chronic problems for a variety of reasons. Biochemistry is complex. Chronic illness affects the individual's biochemical, hormonal and metabolic function. Despite the autonomy of the enteric nervous system, the bowel is connected to the rest of the body and communicates with the whole body. Endocrinopathic and metabolic problems such as hypercalcemia, hypokalemia, hypothyroidism, diabetes and other conditions can contribute to constipation. Treating the underlying condition may help relieve constipation or the necessary treatment may contribute to constipation and other treatment methods may need to be added.

If your cat's constipation is due to Chronic Renal Failure, I highly recommend www.felinecrf.org for comprehensive care.

Transit time can play a role in constipation. Transit time describes how long it takes the food eaten to make the passage through the digestive tube. Unlike a scheduled train system, there is variation in transit time – differences between species, differences between individuals,

 differences influenced by the various foods, fibers and supplements ingested. A cat eating the same diet daily, without food variation, can still experience a change in transit time due to change in schedule, supplements or medications, stress, a vet visit, disruption at home. A temporary shift should not be of great concern, especially if the reason can be determined and corrected, but if the cat's pooping schedule remains off kilter and/or there are hints of digestive upset, it is time to pay close attention.

Diet influences transit time in various ways. The main components of food – protein, fat, carbohydrates – require different digestive processes, some taking longer than others. The fiber content of the diet, the quantity as well as the type of fiber, can play a major role. Soluble fiber tends to delay transit time while insoluble fiber tends to speed transit. But before we jump to conclusions, there is no transit race, no winners or losers. Slower passage may allow more time for absorption of nutrients while increasing transit time may be desirable in some situations. In the natural world, whole foods contain a mix of fibers, the key is balance.

Frequency of eating may also play a role in transit time. Our cats, as a species, naturally eat small frequent meals throughout the 24-hour day. Everything about a cat's physical and metabolic systems evolved around their frequent hunting and feeding pattern and cats function best when this natural pattern is accommodated. Cats are not built to fast, nor are they built to go long hours between meals. Break-fast is a human invention, not a cat invention. It is natural for cats to 'graze' and the physical passage and processing of food helps keep the gut in good shape and form.

Inactivity may play a role in transit time. Movement is life and an inactive cat may tend to have more bowel problems. Of course bowel problems can lessen activity so it is not easy to tell which is the chicken, which is the egg. Still interactive play or a good walk through the house or march around the dining table could be considered as part of a treatment plan.

Dehydration can cause constipation. In dehydration, everything in the body is short of water, including the bowel and the stool. A small creature like a cat can become dehydrated quite quickly from vomiting and/or diarrhea which causes not only water loss but electrolyte loss.

Still an adequately hydrated cat can experience constipation if there is not adequate water retention in the stool itself. Unless water is retained in the stool, unless there is something in the stool that promotes water retention in the stool, the stool will not have sufficient oomph to signal the nerves in the bowel to move it. Water influences stool volume and volume gives a clear signal to the bowel. Unlike the bowel wall and despite live bacterial content, the stool is not a living organism and so is dependent on adequate volume from water content to deliver a proper signal.

Smooth pooping is an elegantly choreographed dance between the stool and the bowel wall. If either partner is out of step or if the rhythm is off or there is a problem with the dance floor or the music, trouble can result.

Pressure of the stool against the bowel wall signals to the bowel that it is time to move its contents. In other words, *the stool invites the bowel to dance.* To extend a proper invitation, the stool needs to be properly formed and sized and of a proper firmness. The proper firmness is a function of the amount of water retained in the stool, not too much, not too little.

Proper poop is like the bed in the story of The Three Bears - Goldilocks wanted a bed that was just right, *not too hard, not too soft.* We want the cat's stool just right - right for a cat stool. A cat's stool is not hard but firmish and not too bulky.

We learned in the chapter on poop that a cat naturally produces a cylindrical segmented stool and that the drier the stool, the more likely the segments will separate during pooping or in the litter box and the smaller each segment may be.

The stool needs to be firm enough to respond to the bowel muscle when the bowel accepts the invitation to dance but not so firm that the stool cannot mold while passing through the anus, which is somewhat less expandable than the rectum. Trying to evacuate too soft a stool can be like pushing a chain or dancing with a rag doll.

The rectum is the poop storage area of the large bowel (large intestine) once the stool is formed, once it is 'done' and ready to exit. A storage area is handy, it allows the pooper to seek a suitable location for pooping, time to get to the litter box or convenient digging hole or to wait until the coast is clear.

The rectum is designed to store stool. *Contrary to common understanding, the stool itself is not toxic while waiting in this storage area, even if several days pass.* If something in the stool is toxic, diarrhea is more likely to result than constipation. The problem with stool not passing in a timely fashion is that more water is withdrawn while it sits, the stool gets smaller and drier and harder, all of which indicates another problem that needs addressing. In addition, more stool is forming behind the accumulated stool if nothing is moving. If the rectum is full, stool begins to accumulate in areas of the large bowel not intended for storage. In a worst case scenario, stool backs up into the small intestine.

Cats have two anal glands, one on either side of the anus, glands which store a strong-smelling secretion whose odor is distinctive for the individual cat. Since cats can't leave sticky notes to communicate, they use scent messages to say, "I was here," and "This is me." When a cat poops, adequate pressure from properly firm poop passing by the anal glands squeezes out a thin coating of the secretion to coat the stool.

If the poop is too soft to stimulate the anal glands when the cat poops, over time the glands' secretions can thicken and harden and the glands become impacted. Impaction is painful and can lead to infection or even rupture of the glands and can cause or complicate constipation. Impacted anal glands themselves are effectively constipated. Impaction requires vet treatment to clear the glands.

If the stool becomes too hard and small and shriveled, newly formed stool can slip down beside present stool and create a traffic jam which may need vet assistance to relieve. Stools in the shape of balls rather than more elongated segments can be very difficult to expel. They keep signaling to the cat that he or she needs to poop but it is as though the ball spins in place or the rectal wall lacks a grip on it. In the final step of stool passage, the anus shortens and pulls up over the stool – if it can.

Different cats will have a stool size normal for that cat but cats are cats and do not produce cow patties or rabbit pellets.

It is important to note changes in the stool that do not relate to other changes, that cannot be accounted for by a change in diet or medication or routine. Be sure to advise your vet of these changes.

The color of stool may provide clues. In the poop chapter, we saw that the normal brown color of stool is due to gut bacterial action on bilirubin. Bilirubin comes from spent red blood cells and is delivered to the gut in bile. Bilirubin has a yellow hue and if the stool passes too quickly, as in diarrhea, before the gut bacteria have their chance, the stool may appear more yellow. If bilirubin is low or absent and the stool has a greenish cast from its bile content, this could indicate a problem with bilirubin excretion and should be reported to the vet. An excessive amount of bilirubin could cause the stool to appear black. Significant changes in stool color which can't be accounted for otherwise indicate need for a vet visit.

A black tarry stool can indicate digested blood from bleeding in the upper gut so the cause must be determined. A stool sample should be checked for occult (hidden) blood. **Remember to distinguish between blood on the stool as opposed to blood in the stool**. Visible blood is called Hematochezia and occult or hidden blood is called Melena. Too often visible blood on the poop in the litter box is reported to the vet or a user group as blood in the stool when it is not mixed in as it would be from a source of bleeding higher up. Visible blood usually indicates a more minor problem low in the bowel, perhaps a little tear or fissure, an indication of straining at stool.

To accept the stool's invitation to dance, the bowel's muscles and nerves need to be in good dance form, supplied with adequate levels of needed nutrients.

"Cats require purity and simplicity." – SEM

- Good blood level of potassium for muscle function
- Good magnesium blood level for nerve function
- All electrolytes and other values in normal range in lab work
- Adequate intake of all the B vitamins to support metabolic functions
- Good quality protein levels to support the carnivorous cat
- Clean fresh water available at all times, not located next to the food bowl
- A proper diet with a cat-suitable source of fiber for the gut bacteria
- A special or prescription diet if the cat requires it

Hypokalemia (low potassium), for example, can cause constipation because muscle tissue needs adequate levels of potassium to function properly. Adequate levels of B vitamins are essential for proper nerve function and other metabolic functions and some conditions, such as Chronic Renal Failure, often result in potassium and B vitamin loss, necessitating supplementation.

Because we see the poop in the litter box, we understandably put most of our focus there but we must not neglect the bowel, the other dance partner. Or the factors the create the music.

A diet lacking appropriate fiber sources for the cat's gut bacteria can lead to constipation.

As we learned in the previous chapter, the SCFAs that the gut bacteria produce not only fuel the bowel wall but also influence the pH of the bowel environment which in turn influences the amount of water the stool retains.

That increase in acidity also helps limit the growth of the more pathogenic gut bacteria whose byproducts are toxic to the cells of the gut wall resulting in inflammation (see more on inflammation below), damage to the enteric nervous system, and negative impact to the Interstitial Cells of Cajal (ICCs) which act as pacemakers in the gut.

Obesity can contribute to constipation. Obesity affects more than weight on the scale, it negatively impacts how everything in the body works. In addition, an obese cat has more difficulty assuming a good squatting position to facilitate pooping.

Various health conditions and medications can affect bowel action and stool formation. Supplements containing iron can cause constipation and can be hard on the gut wall, especially if dosed without food. Please note this is a supplement, an extra, not the iron that is a component of the food in the diet. Iron supplements may also result in a black stool.

Aluminum hydroxide, used as a phosphorus binder in Chronic Renal Failure and other causes of hyper-phosphatemia, can lead to constipation. Aluminum hydroxide may inhibit smooth muscle contraction, as can some other medications. Anything that slows passage, that slows transit time, can increase the time that water can be withdrawn from the stool back into the body. Unless there is something in the diet and/or treatment plan that retains water in the stool, a hard dry shriveled stool can be the result and the cat is constipated. Prevention is key.

Renalzin, a new phosphorus binder coming into the marketplace, contains kaolin in addition to the binder lanthanum carbonate. Kaolin in high doses can cause or contribute to constipation.

Inflammation is the body's initial and innate response to whatever goes wrong, a 911 response to trouble of any kind. Inflammation involves redness, heat, swelling, pain, and impairment or loss of function. Increased blood flow accounts for redness and heat; the body needs to deliver emergency troops to the site and clear the field of debris. Chemical signals stand in for dispatch. Extra white blood cells respond to see what needs to be done and to get busy doing it. We call these troops and the cause and results of their work 'pus' and this accumulation accounts for swelling. Swelling presses on sensitive nerves which is felt as pain. Swelling and presence of extra personnel also limits the ability of the involved tissue or joint or organ to perform its usual functions.

Acute inflammation is, by definition, self limiting. Trouble occurred, the body dealt with it on its own or with treatment, life returns to normal.

Chronic inflammation results in chronic trouble. Inflammation, whether acute or chronic, always involves some 'collateral' damage. Just as fire personnel may chop through a wall to put out the fire to save the house, white blood cells go through cell walls rather than around to reach their targets. The system evolved under the assumption that the damage will be repaired once the emergency is over. If the trouble never resolves, more and more damage occurs and function becomes ever more compromised.

Location of trouble dictates which functions are compromised. An inflamed knee limits bending and walking while an inflamed gut impacts normal absorption of nutrients and compromises the barrier function of the gut wall. Simply put, compromised gut barrier function means what should not get through into the body may get through and what should get through into the body may not get through. Although we cannot readily observe it, the evidence of inflammation is still present – redness, heat, swelling, pain, and impairment or loss of function.

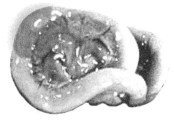

Newer research suggests that the inflammatory response in the gut may send pro-inflammatory products through the mesentery lymphatics into wider circulation and affect distant organs, especially in trauma patients. The same research emphasizes the importance of the use-it-or-lose-it aspects of gut function discussed earlier, that the passage of food itself helps preserve gut barrier function. This is especially important for cats who are naturally frequent feeders. We need to pay special attention to any signs of inappetence. Cats must eat!

Large hairballs which manage to go down the wrong way, the long way, can result in an inflamed or impacted small intestine. Even small hairballs can be difficult to inch along. Formed hairballs are better thrown up on the carpet rather than risk that long journey. While the digestive tract evolved in concert with cats eating furry prey, that fur was consumed with and

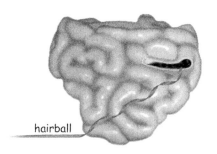

hairball

attached to food. Shed hair ingested during grooming can ball up in the stomach like a load of shoelaces in a washing machine, accumulate and grow too large to pass through the pyloric sphincter. That mass takes up room needed for food but it is a shorter distance to the carpet than the litter box, and a straighter line.

One reader administers a small amount of egg yolk lecithin to her cats daily to reduce the incidence of hairballs. Lecithin has lubricant properties so apparently this practice acts as a 'hair rinse' to prevent swallowed hairs from tangling into a ball in the stomach. Instead the hairs move out with the chyme and eventually land in the litter box in the stool. The reader's dose is 1/6 of a teaspoon daily per cat. She reports that the spoon marked 'dash' in the little sets of measuring spoons labeled pinch, smidgen and dash holds 1/6 of a teaspoon.

The musculature of the healthy large intestine is remarkably strong and under normal conditions performs its job capably without great assistance from voluntary abdominal muscles. The cat assumes the proper squatting position which positions the lower spine and bowel for the best action, contraction of the diaphragm and abdominal muscles is applied and held to exert proper pressure, and the bowel wall does the work. We may think that there's no problem as long as the poop lands in the litter box but seeing signs that the cat is struggling, taking too much time, or needing to apply too much pressure should alert us to potential trouble. The squeezes at the end of pooping shouldn't be confused with abdominal straining.

Constipated humans can, if necessary, sit for long periods on the toilet but a constipated cat can quickly tire from squatting for too long.

The membrane lining of the gut holds receptors, especially abundant in the colon, which respond to stretching and can transmit signals to the brain's vomiting center. The enteric nervous system can run the show on its own but it is still tuned in to the rest of the body. By this stretch receptor mechanism, *straining to poop can result in vomiting* or an overly large stool could cause excessive stretch receptor response.

It is important to work with your vet whenever your cat is experiencing pooping problems in or out of the litterbox. It is not sufficient to note the presence or absence of stool in the litterbox. Is the cat straining to poop? Crying out? Seeking out-of-box places to poop? Not pooping for several days?

There are conditions such as spinal cord injury or congenital malformation which can result in constipation that are beyond the scope of this discussion. Megacolon is also beyond the scope of this discussion but here is a word about the condition. There is a common misunderstanding that megacolon is like an old stretched-out pair of panty hose, that large stools might somehow stretch the bowel out of shape. This is not how things work. Acquired megacolon (as opposed to congenital megacolon or spinal cord injury) can result from damage to the enteric nervous system, damage from neurotoxic byproducts of pathogenic gut bacteria. If there is no nerve action, nothing will move even though the bowel muscle is intact. The problem is not the enlarged portion of the colon but the section which does not allow the stool to pass, does not receive the stool, is no longer dancing. This type of acquired megacolon could be considered a form of peripheral neuropathy.

> *The operative rule of the bowel is: no nerves, no transit.*

Gershon, M. D. The Second Brain:Page 179.
HarperCollins Publishers, Inc., New York, NY.

If damage to the enteric nervous system or to those pacemakers in the bowel, the Interstitial Cells of Cajal, results from malnutrition or toxic bowel conditions or bowel ischemia (decrease in blood flow), the result can be functional bowel disease, problems not with the poop but with the function of the bowel itself.

Incidentally, studies of cats show that many tend to poop in the dark hours of the night. Not all cats, certainly, but there appears to be a circadian rhythm to the act.

It is worth reminding: *Any treatment for constipation, including laxatives and enemas, addresses the water retention in the poop and/or the bowel one way or another.*

:cat_paw: Acute Treatment

The first thing to do if your cat is suffering an acute bout of constipation is to contact the vet.

An acute bout of constipation can occur in a previously healthy cat or a cat with chronic constipation can experience an acute bout.

In a multi-cat household, it can sometimes be difficult to figure out which cat is producing which stool or who is not pooping. One way to sort things out is to feed each cat, in turn, a small amount of baby food beets. Be forewarned that beets may also color the urine, a harmless effect, and that will probably occur more quickly than the beets coloring the stool. Wait a couple of days before giving the beets to the next cat so you are sure whose results are whose.

There are a variety of laxatives on the market. Few of them are suitable for cats. Cats are quirky and sensitive creatures and can all too easily be poisoned by some OTC human treatments. The dailiness of chronic constipation means the treatment needs not only to be effective but very safe over the long term. What might work well enough for occasional treatment may not be suitable for long-term care.

The unique sensitivity of cats as a species means any treatment, whether short or long term, must be especially safe.

Saline Laxatives	Stimulant Laxatives
Saline laxatives are not safe for cats. The term 'saline' includes mineral salts such as magnesium or phosphate salts.	Stimulant laxatives are not suitable for cats.

Aloe Vera   Aloin
Bisacoydl   Cascara Sagrada
Castor Oil   Correctol
Dulcolax   Epsom Salts
Ex-Lax   Magnesium Citrate
Magnesium Sulfate   Milk of Magnesia
Phenolphthalein   Senakot
Senna   Sodium Phosphate

For a cat experiencing an acute bout of constipation, delivering a remedy directly to the rectum may be the best approach, depending on the particular situation. Do, please, heed the emphasized text in the section on Enemas.

If you and your vet have determined that a rectally-delivered remedy is suitable, remember that any object inserted into the anus should be lubricated. Some remedies provide their own lubrication or are pre-lubricated, others require us to lubricate them. Vaseline has been the traditional lubricant but a water-based personal lubricant such as plain K-Y jelly may be a better choice, if on hand, since it more closely mimics the natural lubrication of mucous membranes. Note that only plain lubricants should be used, nothing scented or enhanced, no mint or chocolate flavors, no chemicals added for 'warming' or to 'tingle on contact' please!

Understanding the construction of the anus will make the job of inserting a suitable and suitably lubricated object, whether a suppository or a thermometer, into a cat's anus much easier. The anus has not one but two sphincters. You could think of this as a storm porch on the back of the house. The outer sphincter is under voluntary control, the inner sphincter is not. Normally all traffic is one-way which means the anus does not expect traffic in reverse, something coming in rather than going out, so initially it is a bit of a surprise. Gentle steady pressure causes the outer sphincter to relax, to 'answer the door'. The cat also appreciates this approach. No one wants someone to come busting through the door when a polite but insistent knocking will result in a warmer welcome.

A cold object causes involuntary muscle contraction so prewarm a thermometer, just enough to take the chill off but not enough to affect its reading.

Remember to talk with your cat. Show your cat what you plan to use and explain why and what you plan to do. Talk as from one adult to another, which this relationship is after all. Your cat is an intelligent being and while not every word will be understood, cats pick up on our intent and our intent informs our action. If we think, for instance, that taking a temperature or using a micro-enema requires us to 'shove something up a cat's ass,' that is exactly what we will do with predictably negative results. If, instead, we imagine using gentle steady pressure and visualize gliding in smoothly, that is more likely to happen because our movements will follow. It is far easier to work with a cooperative cat; take the time to elicit cooperation. Cooperation is the kinder and safer approach.

Enemas

Warm water – Body temperature water is quite safe when delivered as a *little* enema, depending on the amount delivered! A cat is a small creature, much smaller than a human. If a cat is constipated, we can assume the rectum is probably occupied by poop and adding too much water stresses the situation further. The point of a warm water enema is not to flush the colon, like preparation for a colonoscopy or bowel surgery, but to increase rectal volume just enough to provide a sufficient signal to the enteric nervous system that something needs to be done. It does not take much water volume to give that signal. Plain warm water will not penetrate or soften the stool well.

If the accumulated stool in the rectum is too large to pass comfortably through the anus in response to the signal, and is rock hard, even a small enema can be very uncomfortable for the cat unless the stool is first softened. A plain water-based personal lubricant product can be added to the water in a 50-50 mix but the total amount of liquid used should be kept small, under 10 ml. A level measuring teaspoon contains 5 ml so less than two level teaspoonsful should be used, a little at a time, not the full amount if the situation is unclear. Remember those stretch receptors in the bowel wall which communicate with the brain's vomiting center?

Too much liquid injected into the bowel may result in your cat vomiting rather than pooping. Start low and go slow!

Feline Pet-ema - Sized for cats and available without prescription, Feline Pet-ema contains Dioctyl Sodium Sulfosuccinate (DSS), a stool softener, in glycerine, with Sorbic Acid as a preservative. Each Feline Pet-ema holds 6 ml of fluid. It is delivered rectally via a prefilled disposable syringe. A stool softener does not work instantly nor necessarily quickly, it takes time to soften stool. The act of inserting anything into the rectum may provide enough stimulus, both in volume increase and nerve stimulation, to trigger action so the syringe tip itself may provoke action. If not, the increased volume from the syringe contents may provoke action. Or the action of the ingredients may do the work over more time. See **Glycerine** and **Stool Softeners** below to understand their action.

Fleet® Liquid Glycerin Enema - FLEET makes a small disposable pre-lubricated enema for human use which contains only glycerin. READ THE LABEL! FLEET also offers saline enemas which should NOT be used for cats. As we learned in Gut 101, the digestive tract is self lubricating but the combination of the insertion of the enema tip, which gives a signal to the ENS, plus the irritant action of glycerin acting on the gut wall, plus the additional volume and lubrication, may help relieve the acute situation. See however the warning about impacted stool. The adult enema contains 7.5 ml which is within reason for a little cat enema but it still may be prudent to deliver only part of the solution initially. The pediatric version contains 4 ml.

Microlax® - Another micro-enema, made by Pharmacia & Upjohn, Microlax® contains sodium citrate dihydrate, sodium lauryl sulfoacetate, glycerin, sorbitol, sorbic acid, and distilled water. Each little enema provides 5 ml of liquid. While not strictly a veterinary product, it is sometimes used in veterinary medicine. Remember that some of the action is triggered by irritation of the mucous membranes. These are not remedies which should be used frequently.

Please note! When using these little enemas, maintain steady pressure on the plunger or especially the bulb when withdrawing the device so that no suction is created. You do not want to exert suction against those tender rectal tissues.

Suppositories

Glycerine - Glycerine acts as an irritant to the gut mucosa and therefore to the ENS, to the nerves in the gut wall,

which kicks them into higher gear. Glycerine is also hygroscopic which means it attracts water to itself making the glycerine even slipperier than normal, providing additional lubrication. As we learned in Gut 101, the digestive tract is self lubricating but the combination of the insertion of the suppository, which delivers a signal to the ENS, plus the irritant action of glycerine acting on the gut wall, plus the additional lubrication may help relieve the situation.

Only the single ingredient glycerine should be used as a suppository, in a pediatric size. Glycerine suppositories can be pared down easily to a smaller size if necessary. You can use a vegetable peeler. Be sure to smooth any rough edges created.

Instead of a glycerine suppository, you can try dipping the end of a Q-tip in liquid glycerine, thoroughly saturating it. Then gently and carefully insert the saturated Q-tip into the rectum and remove it, repeating three or four times. This will not only lubricate the passage but stimulate the voiding reflex.

'Lubricant' Laxatives

Olive oil – Technically a cholagogue (see Glossary), not a lubricant laxative, olive oil has mild laxative properties when a larger dose is given. A larger dose for a cat is a small amount! For a mild bout of constipation, a quarter teaspoonful of olive oil can be given for acute treatment but cats require animal fat sources, not plant oils, so olive oil is not suitable for ongoing care. Olive oil contains terpenic acids and phenolic compounds which a cat's liver are not able to properly detoxify. Some pharmacies carry small bottles of pharmaceutical-grade olive oil. Do not force any oil into the mouth of a cat.

Laxatone and other 'hairball remedies' – Hairball remedies are petrolatum based. Petrolatum, essentially Vaseline, is a more solid cousin of liquid mineral oil. Because oral petrolatum products can deplete fat-soluble vitamins as they pass through the digestive tract, hairball remedies have some vitamins added. Because cats are cats, the remedies are flavored to tempt the cats. On hair, hairball remedies act like creme rinses to keep hair from tangling into a ball although they will not untangle a ball which has already formed. When given as a laxative, the idea is to lubricate the stool. As we know, the gut is self lubricating but additional lubrication may help during an acute bout of constipation.

Petrolatum coats the stool with what we could call a reverse raincoat, a waterproof coating which prevents more water from being resorbed away from the stool into the body, keeping the stool from getting drier and harder and thus making it easier to pass. Several doses of hairball remedy spaced a few hours apart may be enough to get a cat over an acute bout of constipation but these remedies are not a long-term solution and they must travel through the digestive tract to reach their goal. Hairball remedies should never be forced into a struggling cat's mouth. If they are aspirated, they can cause lipoid pneumonia which is difficult to impossible to treat.

Mineral oil – Plain liquid mineral oil should never be delivered orally to a cat. Mineral oil is tasteless and odorless and too easily aspirated into the lungs. This can result in lipoid pneumonia which can be deadly. Do not give a cat liquid mineral oil by mouth.

Lubricant laxatives based on petrolatum are used because, since they are indigestible, they remain in the gut rather than being absorbed into the body as dietary fats/oils. They can be helpful during an acute bout of constipation but are not the most healthful choice for ongoing care for a cat with chronic constipation, they are recommended for short-term use.

As discussed under Suppositories, a glycerine suppository or a Q-tip saturated with liquid glycerine also qualify as lubricant laxatives.

Stool Softeners

Colace contains docusate sodium, a surfactant or wetting agent which makes water 'wetter'. We use the same

 principle when washing greasy pots and pans with dish detergent. Once stool has lost water, it resists rehydration by plain water alone as fatty residues in the stool can render it waterproof – oil and water do not mix. Docusate acts in two ways to relieve constipation. It lowers the surface tension of water which allows water to penetrate hard dry stools, thus increasing volume. This also makes the stools softer and easier to pass, thus reducing straining. Docusate also has a stimulant effect on the gut. It triggers nerve endings in the large intestine and rectum, causing the muscles to contract more often and with greater force which moves the contents of the colon into the rectum and out into the litter box. If the reluctant stool is large, clearly it is better to have the stool softened before it is forced out.

Docusate sodium tastes bitter! If a cat senses a bitter taste, the cat will produce extra saliva and foam at the month in an involuntary attempt to dilute and wash out what is perceived as a toxin. Severe foaming could cause breathing and swallowing difficulties for your cat. Therefore, if a vet approves use of Colace/docusate sodium, avoid the taste and the risk entirely by pilling a Colace capsule, 50 mg. size, and chase the capsule with food or water as discussed in Gut 101 under Esophagus.

Consult your vet!

An oral medication needs to make the trip from mouth to bowel. *Oral stool softeners are not a quick fix, it takes time to rehydrate the stool.*

Osmotic Laxatives

Lactulose – Lactulose is a sweet thick liquid offering an indigestible sugar which acts as an osmotic laxative. In humans it apparently is a fermentable fiber for the gut bacteria. I have read that it is for cats, I have read that it is not. The byproducts of the gut bacteria help regulate pH in the colon, and it is the pH that influences how much water will be retained in the stool. Lactulose alone influences the pH of the bowel, has the necessary slightly acidifying effect to cause water retention thus increasing volume and signaling the ENS. Lactulose requires a prescription from the vet U.S.

Miralax – Miralax, now an OTC drug, is polyethylene glycol, PEG 3350. The number 3350 describes its average molecular weight and distinguishes Miralax from polyethylene 300 or polyethylene 400, for instance. Polyethylene glycol is not propylene glycol, more familiarly called antifreeze. Miralax retains water in the stool or the bowel depending on when it is administered in relationship to meals. See Prevention for more information about Miralax.

Both Lactulose and Miralax are dose-to-effect drugs with a normal stool as the goal. The intent is not to flush out the cat. If the cat has impacted stool, osmotic laxatives are

not suitable until that situation is relieved. We do not want to create pressure behind a dam! In any event, osmotic laxatives do not 'catch up with' the stool already formed to act as stool softeners. They are better used to prevent trouble than to deal with a serious bout of constipation and are not suitable for impacted stool.

Later you'll see a simple colon examination to learn to do at home to better evaluate the situation, or consult your vet to determine current status.

By now, we can see common patterns among these seemingly different approaches. First, they involve water one way or the other, even if that is not apparent on the surface:

• stimulating action by the insertion of a suitable object causes the stool to move sooner rather than later, before it stays put longer and loses even more water
• simply increasing volume in the rectum stimulates action so adding a small amount of a suitably safe liquid may be sufficient, but again observe the caution
• triggering action through stimulation or irritation causes the stool to move sooner rather than later, before it stays put longer and loses even more water
• lubricant laxatives and suppositories irritate and cause stool to move sooner rather than later
• stool softeners allow water to penetrate the stool which increases stool volume which triggers action by signaling to the bowel
• osmotic laxatives draw water in or ensure water retention which increases volume

Laxatives work through common actions – physical and/or chemical stimulation, or volume increase.

We see different brand names, different chemical names, different appliances, but how does the bowel 'see' it?

That question has been answered, in part, in the preceding information. The bowel receives signals through its nervous system, from the pressure of the stool, in the dance we call pooping. In time of need, laxatives can mimic those signals and our goal is to use laxatives that most closely mimic the natural process without going overboard. If a little stimulation will do the job, we do not want to overstimulate.

However, there remains a further problem for us – we have no idea of the situation in the bowel. Is the stool too large to pass easily? A large hard lump that needs softening first? Small shriveled bits unable to initiate bowel action? Is the stool sitting this dance out or has it taken over the lead completely with the bowel trying to keep up?

Remember these illustrations?

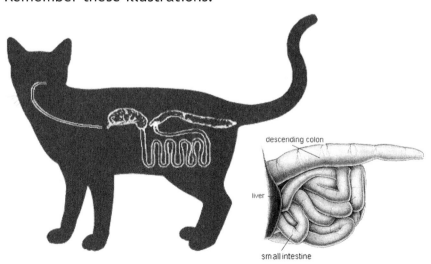

descending colon

liver

small intestine

There is that descending colon, running underneath the cat's spine, behind the ribs and out between the hind legs. That is, in part, what a vet is feeling when he performs an abdominal exam on a cat.

You can learn to feel the contents of the colon, to learn what might be waiting in that chute. Done properly, this will not hurt your cat but you do not want to learn during a time of crisis. If you have another cat in the house, you can practice on the unconstipated cat first. In any event, make this a pleasurable process for both you and your cat or cats. There is no deadline, you can take a week or a month to learn, indulge in a little practice when you and your cat are having a cuddle.

Depending on the girth of the cat, you may be able to reach over the spine with one hand as I could with our slender cat, Jenny Anydots, fingers on one side and thumb on the other, to feel the bowel. With a more generous cat or if your hands are small, you can use one hand on either side of that space behind the ribs and in front of the hind legs. Take your time, your fingers will learn to see, to first find the colon and then to distinguish the muscle of that tube from its contents. We can identify by feel the contents of our pockets or handbag so our hands and brains are well equipped to learn this new application.

The bladder is located toward the ribs and below the colon and does not feel like a tube but like a little balloon with more or less inflation depending on how full of urine it is at the time. Of course you do not want to be putting pressure on the bladder.

You can also feel from the belly side to examine that last section of bowel between the hind legs that exits at the anus. You may even be able to help work out anything waiting right at that door by gently massaging toward the anus.

A manual exploration must be gentle and slow and relaxed. The learning process cannot be rushed and if you are stressed, your cat will only become more stressed. Be sure to explain to your cat what you are doing and why, and report what you learn.

If you feel nothing and yet your cat has not been pooping and you are concerned your cat is constipated, a quick x-ray at the vet's may be necessary to determine whether there is impacted stool higher up in the large bowel. Sometimes absence of evidence is not evidence of absence.

Learning to physically monitor the status of the constipated cat's situation helps us select the best approach and when it is time to head immediately to the vet for assistance.

Once any crisis has passed, it is time to focus on prevention.

In fact it is always time to focus on prevention.

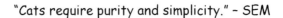

"Cats require purity and simplicity." – SEM

🐾 Prevention of Feline Constipation

Prevention of constipation addresses the retention of water in the poop one way or another.

This theme has been discussed several times and we come back to it again. Water makes the difference between a hard stool and a soft stool. Prevention of constipation means to ensure water retention in the stool, using appropriate methods which benefit the cat in various ways.

The unique sensitivity of cats as a species means any plan, whether short or long term, must be especially safe. Cats are strong, tough little creatures and yet they are very sensitive to diet, medications and household chemicals which may be safe for other species. Each new research study about cats seems to reveal more about their uniquenesses.

Treatment for a cat with a chronic condition needs to be ongoing. *We want to prevent constipation, not chase it.* A cat with chronic tendencies needs a consistent, thoughtful, safe and effective plan to treat and prevent constipation. While the remedies discussed in Acute Treatment can be helpful and some cats may need their ongoing assistance, constipation is not the result of lack of glycerine or stool softeners.

Other healthy cats in the house may have those 'occasional bouts of irregularity' so understanding the digestive tract and constipation prevention can be helpful for them also.

"Cats require purity and simplicity." – SEM

It is not sufficient to see poop in the litter box, we want to support a healthy gut environment.

Diet

Diet is the foundation of health, though not the only factor. Genetics plays a role, as does the cat's life style and exposure to environmental influences.

The details of feline nutrition are outside the scope of this book but health, including gut health, cannot be maintained without good nutrition. Cats have unique nutritional requirements, requirements which differ from humans or dogs or other species. However, the components of the cat's diet do not come from another planet, they are the same components of food which are familiar to us all, the same three pillars of diet – protein, fat and carbohydrate – just as they are for other species including our human selves. Cats require different ratios among those three than another species does but those three pillars are still the foundation of a cat's diet. The sources which fulfill those three pillars need to be selected somewhat differently for cats. For instance, cats require that their protein needs be met primarily by animal rather than plant sources, especially to supply adequate taurine, an amino acid which cats do not synthesize well for themselves. But it is protein, not some peculiar and unique need, that is being met.

Some opine that cats are unable to digest carbohydrates. If cats had not evolved with the ability to digest carbohydrates, the feline pancreas would not produce enzymes to digest carbohydrates and the feline pancreas does produce those enzymes. *Cats do not produce salivary amylase but they do produce pancreatic amylase.* Whole natural foods, including a mouse, are a mix of protein, fat and carbohydrate. The word 'carbohydrate' is a technical term in nutritional language; it is not synonymous with 'veggies' or 'grains'.

The question is not whether cats can digest carbohydrates, they can. The question is, what are appropriate carbohydrate sources for cats and what ratio is appropriate in their diet. We often read that cats do not require carbohydrates, which is true from one angle, cats themselves can manage without carbohydrate content in the diet. But not requiring does not mean cats are unable to digest carbohydrates.

Because cats utilize protein and fat so well to run and support their bodies and maintain their blood sugar levels, little to nothing is left over for the gut bacteria when the diet consists solely of protein and fat. *The cat's native diet of mouse and other small prey was not just protein and fat; a mouse offers about three percent carbohydrate and the mouse digestive tract contains some plant material.* Something needs to be included in the diet for the cat's gut bacteria, some form or part of plant material. The chapter Gut Bacteria and Fiber covers the benefits in some depth.

If only protein leftovers are available for gut bacteria to ferment, the more pathogenic bacteria benefit at the expense of the beneficial gut bacteria. Those protein leftovers come from shed gut wall cells and recirculating waste products from protein metabolism as well as any undigested dietary protein.

Keeping the beneficial bacteria populations high means they can convert the nitrogenous (protein) waste products into themselves, into more friendly bacterial bodies made of protein, which prevents the more toxic protein waste products from harming the gut wall. Better the friendly bacteria proliferate than those who are less desirable.

The point of fiber is that it is not digestible by the eater, whether that eater is a cat or a human, and so the undigested fiber remains in the digestive tract and flows on to the gut bacteria waiting in the wings. The parts of the included plant material that are digestible will be digested and utilized by the cat herself and, *since cats have low dietary carbohydrate requirements, what to include is more critical for cats than for us omnivorous humans who can safely eat a much wider variety of plant foods in greater quantity.*

Fiber or Prebiotics

The common term used for fiber naturally contained in food is dietary fiber. Fiber sources such as psyllium, FOS (fructooligosaccharides), inulin, beet pulp fiber, chicory root extract, etc. are called functional fibers. The dividing line is not all that clear since functional fibers may be extracted or concentrated from foods or may be synthesized.

Fiber is termed a prebiotic because it feeds the probiotics which is another word for gut bacteria. The term 'prebiotic' is usually reserved for functional fiber products. Few of us eat our baked squash or dark green leafy vegetables and then announce we just ate some prebiotics.

Ideally the chosen diet provides adequate and suitable fiber content but some cats may need additional help. Fiber sources should be appropriate for cats and feed the beneficial gut bacteria without overfeeding them.

Cats, or rather their gut bacteria, do better with low-to-moderately fermentable fiber sources. Commercial cat food companies have access to fiber sources which we may not have. Research has shown that *beet root fiber* and *rice bran* are good fiber sources for cats; they preferentially feed the beneficial gut bacteria and are not highly fermentable so do not risk bacterial overgrowth. Note that rice bran is a source of phosphorus if limiting phosphorus is necessary for your cat. There are about 11 milligrams of phosphorus in 1/8 teaspoon of rice bran though not all the phosphorus is bioavailable. All foods contain some phosphorus.

Guar gum is a common fiber source in commercial canned cat foods and in one study was more highly fermentable than other choices such as beet fiber and rice bran. Some fiber sources such as cellulose and psyllium starve the beneficial bacteria.

Many of us now read the back label of cat food, to choose cat food more carefully, but the type of fiber listed is still an orphan topic. It should not be, fiber is equally important in the dietary scheme even if it does not feed the cat directly.

Dietary Fiber

Pumpkin or Other Winter Squash – A traditional vet recommendation and a good one, plain unspiced canned pumpkin can help relieve either constipation or diarrhea as it normalizes the situation. The beneficial gut bacteria, when properly fed, are good at normalizing the bowel environment. Some cats report that Libby's plain canned pumpkin is the preferred brand but canned pumpkin does not agree with all cats. Baked winter squash can be fed and your cat may have preferences as to type of squash, or baby food winter squash can be used. Use small amounts mixed into several of the daily meals, a small amount being 1/4 to 1/2 teaspoon. Then monitor the results. Remember this is food for the gut bacteria, not the cat himself. If using canned pumpkin, freeze the can contents in ice cube trays, pop the frozen cubes into a freezer container, then thaw a cube at a time in a little glass jar in the fridge. Although cats are unable to convert the beta-carotene in orange vegetables to Vitamin A as humans can, they nevertheless utilize beta-carotene for their own health purposes.

Green Beans – Many cats like green beans, either home cooked, canned or baby food green beans. Some cats enjoy fresh raw green beans. Again, use small amounts mixed into several of the daily meals or offered separately at mealtimes.

Peas – Many cats also like peas which can be used in similar fashion to pumpkin/squash and green beans.

Slippery Elm Bark Powder – Familiarly called SEB, slippery elm bark is an old folk remedy for digestive problems. SEB has a reputation of being soothing to mucous membranes, which as we remember line any organ that has a direct connection to the outer world. SEB also contains fermentable fiber. There are two ways of using SEB, as a syrup and as the powder. SEB powder can be purchased from the bulk herb section of a health food store and an ounce or two goes a long way. Capsules of SEB must contain flow agents in order to get the capsules filled, to keep the powder from flying to the ceiling, so purchase bulk powder if you can. To provide fermentable fiber, use very small amounts of the powder in several meals. Remember this is dry powder so more concentrated than the fiber sources above. Start with 1/16 teaspoon or less and monitor results. To make the syrup, sprinkle a teaspoon of the powder over a cup of cool water in a little saucepan. Let the powder sit until it is wetted, this will avoid lumps to stir out. Then heat over medium heat, stirring the while, until the syrup is translucent and thickened a bit. It will thicken more as it cools. Store in a clean lidded glass jar in the fridge. Of course these amounts can be halved and there is no precise recipe, you can adjust the amount of powder per measure of water. SEB syrup keeps about a week in the fridge as long as the contents have not been contaminated by unclean utensils. Since it is easy to make, it is better to dump if there is any question and to mix up a new batch. Give 1 or 2 mls two or three times a day by mouth or mix into food.

Grass – Growing 'cat grass' indoors has become quite popular, for those cats who have no outdoor access, lack access to safe grass outdoors, or experience long grassless winters. Grass contains fiber, not only in the grass itself but in its juice. Cats know a thing or two. Grass growing kits are widely available but for the definitive site on growing your own cat grass, see www.weirdstuffwemake.com/ sweetwatergems/cats/catgrass.html.

Catnip – While catnip is not usually a daily event in cat lives and we do not add it to meals as a fiber source, nor is every cat genetically predisposed to appreciate catnip, catnip nonetheless contains fiber. In addition, catnip has a historic reputation as helpful for digestive upsets in humans, catnip tea in the human case. Part of the lore of catnip is its relaxant effect on the bowel. Source dry catnip with as much care as you would cat food or consider growing your own, for cats to nibble fresh or for you to dry to offer in off season. Select a mature sturdy plant from a nursery, one that can hold up to the assault of eager cats, or be prepared to protect it until it grows up. Catnip, whether dry or fresh, retains its properties but there is a difference in quality among the various producers of dry catnip. Since cats eat catnip as well as roll in it, you want a good source.

Changes to the diet or routine of a cat should be made gradually, to allow the cat to adjust and to permit the digestive tract to adapt. Cats sometimes need a new item or routine to be introduced several times before they accept. A tiny smidge of pumpkin can be added to a meal, the amount on the end of a toothpick or fork tine, not to fool the cat but to introduce gradually. There is no advantage to trying to push the process and good reasons not to rush the process. Nothing given can be retrieved but the amount can be increased tomorrow. Monitor the cat and the litter box during this process. These fiber sources are not systemic medications which means there is no precise dose nor is each cat eating the same diet with exactly the same other fiber sources.

Although I have read no research to confirm this idea, I think rotating these extra fiber sources may be a good plan. We have all heard that old cliche, that variety is the spice of life, and there is no reason to think otherwise for gut bacteria. Before cat food came in a bag or can, a cat ate a varied diet of creatures who ate varied diets which provided a varied diet for the cat's gut bacteria. If one dietary fiber source is introduced to a cat who seems to need extra fiber to prevent constipation and that fiber seems to 'stop working', try rotation.

Functional Fiber

Inulin, Psyllium, FOS (Fructooligosaccharides), etc. - Follow the manufacturer's instructions. Not all of these fiber sources are fermentable by cats, which starves their gut bacteria if serving as the only fiber source, and some are too fermentable or do not preferentially feed the more beneficial bacteria. As stated earlier, it is not sufficient to see poop in the litter box, we want to support a healthy gut environment. Research in the future, research specific to cats, will help refine the complex subject of functional fiber, of concentrated fiber sources extracted from foods.

Probiotics

A term for supplements of beneficial bacteria, probiotic supplements proliferate in the marketplace, for pets and for humans. Every choice advertises itself as the best choice. Research in this field truly is still in its infancy compared to how much there is yet to learn. Unless the cat has been on antibiotics or has some other specific health condition that indicates a need for probiotic supplements, my reasoning suggests that feeding appropriate fiber to the cat's resident gut bacteria makes more sense. After all, they already live there so are native residents, and may be suffering due to lack of feeding. Since half or more of the dry matter weight of the poop is gut bacteria, feeding the cat's own gut bacteria with suitable fiber makes sense from that angle, too. We could think of the gut bacteria as a chicken coop. It does no good to bring in ever more chickens if none of them is being fed. If you think your cat appears to require a probiotic supplement, work with your vet.

Recent research brings up the question as to whether live or killed probiotic supplements are better and safer. Those of us familiar with probiotic supplements have assumed that live bacteria are needed, we want to see so many million live organisms per acre stated on the bottle. While it is too early to know what research will eventually show, it is good to know there is a legitimate question as to the safety of live probiotics and may, surprisingly, show benefits from killed sources to which the gut responds. This suggests an additional reason for feeding the cat's own bacteria thoughtfully before reaching for an unnecessary supplement, and for working with one's vet when a supplement appears necessary.

Vitamins and Minerals

Muscle needs good potassium blood levels to function properly, to respond to signals and intentions, to maintain oomph.

Nerves need B vitamins and adequate magnesium blood levels to transmit signals properly.

Nerve sheaths, the outer protective covering of nerves, need good body levels of Vitamin B12 to ensure nerve integrity, so that the nerves inside the sheaths are not vulnerable to exposure and do not 'short out' as it were. The usual form of supplemental B12, added to most commercial cat foods and supplements, is cyanocobalamin which requires conversion in the body to an active form. Cyanocobalamin is actually an artifact of the purification process when synthesizing Vitamin B12. The methylcobalamin form of Vitamin B12 does not require the same conversion and is now more readily available for purchase, for cats who require supplemental Vitamin B12.

The entire family of B vitamins called B Complex are important to help maintain gut health and to prevent constipation. Vitamins are not nutrients, they are coenzymes, that is they assist enzymes to do their jobs.

Enzymes are not only involved in digestion, enzymes play a role in all metabolic functions and each enzyme is specific to its task. Without adequate B vitamins such as folic acid and Vitamin B12, enzymatic function suffers. First to suffer are those areas of the body with faster cellular turnover such as the gut wall and the blood components. If gut barrier function is reduced, the body itself is more vulnerable to trouble and the enteric nervous system is at risk of damage.

Of course general nutrition is important which a good diet supplies in a balanced format. Extra vitamins and minerals seem to be added to everything commercial made for the cat, from treats to 'appetizers', and many humans who live with cats think that a cat needs a daily vitamin/mineral supplement in addition to the diet. Unless a cat tests deficient, is not eating well, or has a condition that requires extra supplementation, more is not better than enough and may be harmful. The B vitamins are water soluble and so more 'forgiving' as any extra can more easily be dumped into urine rather than accumulating in the body. Still unnecessary supplementation, above demonstrated or diagnosed need, is to be avoided.

Food itself is very nutritious. Before humans came along to invent supplements, every living being on earth was sustained by food, for millions of years, and despite dire warnings to the contrary, food is still nutritious. A stroll through the USDA National Nutrient Database is surprisingly reassuring, in a general sense, about the nutritional value of food items such as meats or the vegetables listed above for dietary fiber. www.nal.usda.gov/fnic/foodcomp/search

I have found that both diet and nutrition make more sense when I think of food as having had a previous life. While that is not always a comfortable mental process, it is nevertheless true that items we come to call food once had lives of their own, whether that was an animal life or a plant life, a chicken or a squash. Chickens and squashes have nutritional requirements of their own which are similar to ours in many ways even though they may use different tactics to meet those needs. Squash fruits do not need skeletons, they need strong cell walls to form a sturdy incubator for their seeds. Take a moment to check out 'squash, winter' at the database above, read the list of nutrients and realize that the squash plant was using potassium and magnesium and calcium and phosphorus and B vitamins and amino acids and lipids for its own nutritional agenda, just as we do for ours and cats do for theirs. Squashes go about their business quietly but they still have personal business which requires nutrition.

The listings at that site for the various food plants focus on nutrients of interest to us, the human eaters, but there is more to plants than what we humans find important for the dinner table. Unlike ourselves and our cats, plants are not able to sock a predator in the nose or run and hide so they developed various ways to protect themselves including thick hides, thorns, and chemical warfare.

If you would like to learn more about the complexity of plant chemistry, check out Dr. Duke's Phytochemical and Ethnobotanical Databases at www.ars-grin.gov/duke/ to understand why we need to choose plant sources more carefully for carnivorous cats than for omnivorous humans. We ate a large variety of plant foods and evolved with livers which are capable of detoxifying many more plant chemicals than cats can detoxify. Cats, who ate little plant material directly, depended on the livers of their prey species to do the detoxifying for them, then ate the prey. Either cats never developed the necessary hepatic pathways or lost them along the evolutionary trail. We need to select dietary plant material more carefully for cats.

Osmotic Laxatives

If a change in diet or the addition of appropriate fiber to the diet is not enough to prevent constipation in a cat prone to constipation, osmotic laxatives can be helpful so they are included in this prevention chapter also. Consult with your vet for the best choice and dose for your cat.

•**Miralax** – Miralax is polyethylene glycol, PEG 3350. The number 3350 describes its average molecular weight and distinguishes Miralax from polyethylene 300 or polyethylene 400, for instance. *Polyethylene glycol is not propylene glycol, more familiarly called antifreeze. Polyethylene glycol is also not ethylene glycol. It is polyethlene glycol. The differences in chemical formulas matter.* We would be pleased to drink a cool glass of H_2O (water) but should not be pleased to drink H_2O_2 (hydrogen peroxide) even though there is only a single atom of oxygen difference per molecule. Miralax retains water in the bowel and/or the stool. Miralax is a powder which readily dissolves in water or wet food. A typical starting dose for a cat is 1/8 teaspoon total daily, divided into several smaller portions over the course of the day, but your vet should advise for your cat.

There is a warning on the Miralax bottle for kidney patients which unnerves many with cats with kidney disease. That warning is present not because Miralax is harmful for kidney patients, it is not harmful. Now that Miralax is an OTC product, no longer requiring a prescription, it is a caution for humans with a tendency to self-diagnose and self-treat for months without consulting with a doctor, humans who think if a little is good, a lot is better. Provoking the equivalent of diarrhea by use of any laxative causes water and electrolyte loss which can lead to dehydration which is more risky for those with kidney disease than for healthy individuals. Proper and appropriate use of Miralax is safe for cats with kidney disease, with emphasis on proper and appropriate, with a normal stool as the goal.

Lactulose - Lactulose is an indigestible sugar that acts as an osmotic laxative. In humans it apparently is a fermentable fiber for the gut bacteria. I've read that it is for cats, I've read that it isn't. The byproducts of the gut bacteria help regulate pH in the colon, and it is the pH that determines how much water will be retained in the stool. Lactulose alone influences the pH of the bowel, it has the necessary slight acidifying effect to cause water retention, whether or not it is fermentable by cats. Lactulose requires a prescription from the vet who will also prescribe the recommended starting dose for your cat. Lactulose, like Miralax, is a dose-to-effect drug with a normal stool as the goal.

Concerns are often expressed about cats with chronic constipation, such as cats with kidney disease, that use of an osmotic laxative will dehydrate the cat because these products draw water to the bowel or hold it in the stool. If producing a normal stool puts a cat at risk of dehydration, more is wrong than constipation and sometimes what is wrong is the human reasoning. Dehydration is not a recommended treatment for constipation! *The amount of water needed to normalize the stool in response to an osmotic laxative is the same amount of water by any other method including diet and dietary fiber.* This does not mean that these osmotic laxatives should not be treated with respect, of course they should be used conservatively and appropriately. But producing a normal stool by use of an osmotic laxative should not dehydrate a cat.
Again, all changes for the cat should be made gradually, to allow the cat to adjust and to permit the digestive tract to adapt. The digestive tract is remarkably adaptable, within certain parameters, but it takes time to adapt.

Remember, increasing Miralax or Lactulose increases the amount of water in the bowel/stool. If the stool is too soft, reduce the amount of laxative. Osmotic laxatives are dose-to-effect drugs and, unlike most medications, we can monitor the effects in the litter box.

Here, in summary, are the CliffsNotes for this book:

• inside the gut is not inside the body
• the difference between a hard stool and a soft stool is water in the stool
• prevention of constipation involves water one way or the other, water retained in the poop, not necessarily in the cat
• since they are on our side, we honor gut bacteria with suitable fiber
• there is more to treating and preventing constipation than seeing poop in the litter box, we want to support and maintain gut health
• cats are quirky, sensitive and astonishing and we love them

🐾 Glossary

• Absorption – the process by which nutrients from digested food move from the gut into the body and how cells exchange nutrients and water with the blood stream
• Absorption, Passive – osmosis, a selective diffusion process [see Osmosis]
• Active Transport – requires energy and a specific carrier molecule
• Adenosine Triphosphate (ATP) – a chemical synthesized by the mitochondria in cells to produce energy
• Amino Acids – the 'building blocks' of protein; protein is constructed of chains of amino acids which are folded into complex arrangements
• Artery – a blood vessel which carries oxygenated blood away from the heart
• Arteriole – the smallest division of the arteries
• ATP - [see Adenosine Triphosphate]
• Bacterial Translocation – gut bacteria or their byproducts moving across the gut wall barrier into circulation
• Barrier Function – active function of the gut wall which protects and limits access to the inner body
• Bile – a digestive juice secreted by the liver and stored in the gall bladder; bile emulsifies fats [see Emulsify]

• Brush Border – an apt term for an epithelial surface covered with microvilli [see Epithelium and Microvilli]
• Carnivore, Carnivorous – species who eats mainly other animals
• Cecum – a blind pouch at the beginning of the large intestine
• Central Nervous System – the brain and spinal cord
• Cholagogue – a drug or other substance which promotes the discharge of bile from the gall bladder, purging it downward
• Chyle – milky mix of emulsified dietary fat and lymph [see Bile, Emulsify, and Lymph]
• Chyme – thick semifluid mass of partly digested food made in the stomach
• Circulatory System – a system for delivery and pickup
• CNS - see Central Nervous System
• Colon – a term for the large bowel or large intestine
• Detoxify - to remove or to make safe, said of chemicals and poisons
• Diffusion, Facilitated – diffusion requiring a carrier but not usually an energy source
• Diffusion, Passive – movement of molecules or ions from an area of high concentration to an area of lower concentration
• Digestion – the processes, both mechanical and chemical, by which food is broken down into absorbable form [see Absorption]
• Digestive System – the digestive tract plus the internal organs of pancreas, liver and gall bladder [see Digestive Tract]
• Digestive Tract – a complex specialized tube running from mouth to anus; the outside-the-inner-body part of the Digestive System
• Duct – a tubular channel used to deliver a secretion or substance

• Duodenum – the first section of the small intestine where the chyme is neutralized by buffers from the pancreas and bile delivered from the gall bladder

• Electrolytes – dissolved ions, usually of minerals, that conduct electrical impulses which facilitate movement in and out of cells

• Emulsify – to create a suspension of two substances, like oil and water, that would normally not mix

• Endocrine – glands in the body, such as the thyroid, pituatary, pancreas, which secrete hormones directly into the blood stream to give orders and directions elsewhere

• Endocrinopathic – trouble in the endocrine gland system, too much hormone production, too little hormone production [see Hormone]

• Endocytosis – absorption by engulfing [see Pinocytosis and Phagocytosis]

• ENS – [see Enteric Nervous System]

• Enteric Nervous System – a subdivision of the Peripheral Nervous System that directly controls the gastrointestinal system

• Enzymes - biomolecules constructed of amino acids that speed up biochemical reactions without themselves changing in the process

• Epithelium – tissue which covers a surface or lines an organ and is composed of cells which secrete or transport or regulate; the skin (epidermis) is one form of epithelium

• Feces – see Poop

• Fermentable Fiber – fiber which the gut bacteria can utilize

• Fiber – undigestible/nonabsorbable leftovers from plant digestion consisting of mainly complex sugar molecules

• Fiber, Dietary – fiber naturally present in food ingredients

• Fiber, Functional – fiber added to food items

• Fiber, Soluble – fiber which can dissolve in water

• Fiber, Insoluble – fiber which does not dissolve in water

• Gall Bladder - storage organ for bile synthesized in the liver
• Gastric Acid – a very acidic solution composed mainly of hydrochloric acid secreted into the stomach by special glands
• Gland – A cell or group of cells or organ that produces a secretion for use elsewhere
• Goblet Cells – specialized cells whose sole function is to secrete mucin which dissolves in water to form mucous (see Mucous)
• Gut Bacteria – microscopic organisms living in the bowel in n umbers which outnumber the cells of the body
•Hematochezia – visible bright red blood on the stool [see Melena]
• Hepatic – of the liver, involving the liver
• Hormone – a chemical which controls and regulates the activily of certain cells or organs
• Ileocecal Valve – the valve between the small intestine and the large intestine (see Sphincter)
• Ileum – last section of the small intestine where absorption of Vitamin B12 and resorption of bile salts occurs and whose wall contains an abundance of Peyer's Patches
• ICC – [see Interstitial Cells of Cajal]
• Infection – inflammation in response to foreign invasion by bacteria or other invasive organisms (see Inflammation and Pus)
• Inflammation – the body's innate and initial response to injury or other troubles characterized by pain, heat, redness, swelling and possible impairment of function (see Pus and Infection)
• Interstitial Cells of Cajal – cells in the wall of the gut that act as pacemakers for movement contractions, that set the pace of action
• Interstitial Fluid – the body's fluid outside the blood vessels

- Involuntary – not under one's own control
- Jujenum – longest and middle section of the small intestine where most absorption of nutrients occurs
- Lacteal – the chyle collecting vessel in the middle of each villus [see Chyle and Villi/Villus}
- Laxative – a food or drug that facilitates pooping
- Leukocytes – white blood cells
- Lumen – the interior space of a tubular organ such as an intestine or blood vessel
- Lymph – interstitial fluid once that fluid has moved into the lymph system [see Interstitial Fluid]
- Melena – occult or hidden blood mixed into the stool from a bleed higher in the digestive tract, often resulting in a dark tarry stool [see Hematochezia]
- Mesentery – tissue constructed of folds of the peritoneum which supports the small intestine like a flexible scaffolding and carries the blood supply to the small intestine for absorption and transport of nutrients
- Mesocolon – the mesentery of the large intestine [see Mesentery]
- Metabolism, Metabolic – body processes at the cellular level
- Microvilli – smaller villi covering the villi
- Mitochondria – the power generators of a cell, power used to fuel cell division, absorption, etc. [see Adenosine Triphosphate or ATP]
- Molecule – the smallest particle of a substance that retains the chemical and physical properties of the substance and is composed of two or more atoms. A molecule of water is an example; two atoms of hydrogen and one of oxygen forms a molecule of water.
- Monocyte – a phagocytic white blood cells [see Phagocyte]
- Mucin – a substance composed of glycosylated proteins emitted by the goblet cells which forms mucous in contact with water [see Goblet Cells and Mucous]

• Mucous or Mucus – buffered slippery secretion of mucous membrane, a gel which lubricates and protects the membranes themselves and plays a role in immune function at the local level
• Mucous (or Mucus) Membrane – mucous-secreting tissue lining all body passages that lead to the outer world
• Muscle – specialized tissue with the ability to contract and to conduct electrical impulses
• Neutrophil – a phagocytic white blood cell [see Phagocyte]
• Omnivore, Omnivorous – species who eat both animal and plant foods
• Organ – a fully differentiated structural and functional unit in an animal that is specialized for some particular function
• Osmosis – diffusion of water across a selectively permeable membrane
• Pepsin – a protyletic (protein digesting) enzyme produced by special cells in the stomach to initiate protein digestion
• Peripheral Nervous System - the nerves belonging to other than the Central Nervous System and the Enteric Nervous System
• Peristalsis – the rhythmic rippling motion of muscles in the digestive tract to move its contents along [see Segmentation]
• Peritoneum – the membrane lining the body cavity
• Peyer's Patches – patches of lymphoid tissue or lymphoid nodules especially prevalent on the wall of the ileum which contain large amounts of lymphocytes and other cells of the immune system
• pH – a measure of how acid or alkaline a solution is
• Phagocyte - white blood cells whose assignment is to move out of the blood into tissue or lymph to destroy bacteria or consume debris
• Phagocytosis – absorption by 'eating' large molecules [see Endocytosis]

- Pinocytosis – absorption by 'sipping' small water soluble molecules [see Endocytosis]
- Plicae Circulares – folds of the inner lining of the small intestine
- PNS - see Peripheral Nervous System
- Poop – familiar term for waste material discharged from the bowel
- Probiotics – supplement of beneficial live microorganisms such as bacteria and yeasts
- Pus – the hallmark of inflammation, a mix of white blood cells, fluid from damaged cells, and cellular debris (see Infection and Inflammation)
- Pyloric Sphincter – the valve between the stomach and the small intestine (see Sphincter)
- Rectum – the poop storage area of the large bowel
- Resorb or Resorption – to absorb again [see Absorption], essentially a reversal of direction
- Rugae – series of ridges produced by folding of the wall of an organ. Think origami. The stomach wall is folded into rugae, it is not smooth like a bowling ball.
- Saliva – a mix of mucous, water, enzymes and electrolytes which serves to lubricate food's passage down the esophagus as well as cleansing and protecting the mouth
- Segmentation – mixing contractions of the digestive tract; works in concert with peristalsis
- Septicemia – toxic systemic bacterial infection
- Short Chain Fatty Acids (SCFAs) – fermentation byproducts of gut bacteria
- Smooth Muscle – type of muscle in the gut wall as opposed to striated muscle; involuntary muscle
- Sphincter/Valve – a ring of muscle that contracts to close an opening and relaxes to open
- Striated Muscle – skeletal muscle (voluntary) and heart muscle (involuntary)
- Stool – see Poop

• Synthesize – to make something new out of different parts, whether a chemical or a rag rug or a casserole from leftovers

• Translocation – change of location; gut bacterial breach of the barrier of the gut wall into the blood stream

• Valve – see Sphincter

• Vein – a blood vessel that carries deoxygenated blood back to the heart for reoxygenation

• Venule – the smallest division of the veins

• Villi (plural) and Villus (singular) – literally "shaggy hair", fingerlike projections on the wall of the small intestine, each covered in turn with microvilli

• Voluntary – under one's own control

• Water – the original, and still the most widely used, solvent; indispensable in poop to prevent constipation

"Cats require purity and simplicity." – SEM

🐾 Review – Pinning The Tails On That Donkey

© Pat Erickson 2009

Introduction
• Note that straining to urinate could be confused with straining at stool. A cat who is unable to urinate is experiencing a medical emergency and must be seen by a vet immediately.
• The best treatment for a constipated cat is a human who understands how things work.
• This information is not a substitute for proper veterinary diagnosis and treatment.

The First Lesson
• The inside of the tube called the digestive tract is not inside the body.
• For the eater, the gut wall is the first line of defense between the outside world and the inside of the body.
• Swallowing food gets food into the digestive tract, into the gut, not into the body. Before food can be put to use in the body, it needs to be digested and then absorbed into the body.

Gut 101
• The digestive tract starts at the mouth and ends at the anus with the esophagus, the stomach, the small intestine, and the large intestine in between, all hooked together in a long continuous complex tube.
• The digestive system includes organs that actually are inside the body but work closely with the digestive tract – the liver, the gall bladder and the pancreas.
• The digestive tract is self-lubricating.
• The gut wall is composed of smooth muscle cells whose action is involuntary.
• The enteric nervous system is a huge affair; its cells make up a majority of the peripheral nervous system!
• Food provides the nourishment needed by the body to fuel, build, repair and maintain itself and all its parts.
• Before food can nourish, it must be digested so it can be absorbed into the body.
• Food that does not remain in the mouth is not available to ferment in the mouth.
• Many people are surprised by the length of the esophagus.
• For cats, all solid medications and supplements should be 'chased' with sufficient food or water to ensure they make the long journey successfully and do not become entrapped in the esophagus. Chasing liquid medications is also a nice courtesy to avoid potential irritation of the tender mucosa.
• Enzymes break down larger molecules into smaller and smaller molecules.

Gut 102
• The small intestine is a creatively ruffled affair.
• The mesentery is an elegant evolutionary development, a membrane that not only anchors the small intestine yet still allows flexibility of the organ plus provides pick-up-and-delivery service for all those nutrients that are being released from the food.

"Cats require purity and simplicity." – SEM

• Immediately after the chyme arrives in the duodenum, the acid from the stomach is neutralized by a buffer.
• Enzymes from the pancreas are delivered to the duodenum to digest carbohydrates, fats, and to complete the digestion of protein.
• Bile, synthesized by the liver and stored in the gall bladder, enters into the duodenum via the bile duct to emulsify edible fats present in the chyme, resulting in a milky mix called chyle.
• The neutralized chyme flows through the small intestine like a slow swirling river, propelled along by both peristalsis and segmentation.
• As the chyme swirls and flows through the jejunum, molecules of digested nutrients contact the villi and are absorbed via the mesentery into the blood system for distribution to all parts of the body where they are put to use.
• Digestion breaks bigger pieces into smaller and smaller pieces. Mechanical digestion uses physical means to break big pieces down, for greater surface area and better enzymatic access. Chemical digestion employs enzymes to snip the small pieces into smaller molecules by breaking chemical bonds that hold compounds together.
• On and between these folds are millions of tightly packed little fingerlike projections called villi.
• Not only do the villi and their microvilli expand the inner surface area of the small intestine, they also serve as loading docks and gateways.
• There may be 6,000 to 25,000 villi per square inch of intestinal wall, depending on the species whose intestine it is and the particular section of the intestine.
• Just as the theme in digestion is to break big bits into smaller and smaller bits, a circulatory system has a similar theme, working from big through little, littler and littlest, down to the microcirculation level, and circulating back up through small to big again.

• A circulatory system functions as a pick-up-and-delivery system; the system can pick up, transport, and deliver useful and necessary goods or pick up, transport, and dump the waste.

• The smallest blood vessels are not built to withstand the initial pressure of a heartbeat sending blood coursing through the arteries so blood pressure in the little capillaries is much less than blood pressure in the major arteries.

• Capillaries are the key to absorption of nutrients into the circulatory systems.

• Goblet cells emit mucin which in contact with water forms mucous.

• Nutrients are absorbed from the fluid environment of the lumen into the internal fluid environment of the villi where they are picked up by the villi's blood or lymph capillaries and thus into their respective circulatory systems.

• Absorption is not a single process but different strategies depending on what is to be absorbed. There are several possibilities or a combination of strategies.

• Leukocyktes are white blood cells and the villi are well stocked, especially with phagocytes like neutrophils and monocytes who attack potential invaders and gobble up debris.

• Communication between the ENS and the gut occurs across the lining of the gut without the ENS physically entering the lumen.

• The health of the cat depends on the health of the villi who themselves depend on good nutrition and nonexposure to toxic substances. Villi also require the physical passage of food in a use-it-or-start-to-lose-it response.

• The small intestine evolved to transport liquidy contents, not solid objects . . . such as formed hairballs.

• The large bowel makes poop out of soup!

• The large intestine or bowel is also where fermentable dietary fiber in the chyme is fermented by the trillions of gut bacteria who live in the bowel.
• Pressure from the poop, moving into the rectum and pressing from the inside out on the nervous system of the bowel, the enteric nervous system, signals the bowel when it is time to move.

Water
• The problem of constipation is not necessarily lack of water in the cat, it is lack of water retention in the stool.

Gut Bacteria and Fiber
• Food feeds the cat. Fiber feeds the gut bacteria. And the gut bacteria play an important role in helping to prevent constipation as well as maintaining the health and integrity of the gut wall.
• The SCFAs produced by the beneficial gut bacteria help maintain the pH of the stool in the slightly acidic range which helps to retain water in the stool. Water retention in the stool is a function of chemistry.

Poop
• Poop is not leftover food.
• The more water retained in the poop, the softer the poop. The less water, the harder the poop.
• Any treatment for constipation, including laxatives and enemas, addresses the water retained in the poop and/or present in the large bowel one way or another.

What Goes Wrong?
• Transit time can play a role in constipation.
• Diet influences transit time in various ways.
• Frequency of eating may also play a role in transit time.
• Inactivity may play a role in transit time.

• Dehydration can cause constipation.
• Smooth pooping is an elegantly choreographed dance between the stool and the bowel wall.
• The stool invites the bowel to dance.
• Proper poop is like the bed in the story of The Three Bears – not too hard, not too soft.
• The stool needs to be firm enough to respond to the bowel muscle when the bowel accepts the invitation to dance, but not so firm that the stool cannot mold while passing through the anus.
• Contrary to common understanding, the stool itself is not toxic while waiting in this storage area, even if several days pass.
• If the poop is too soft to stimulate the anal glands when the cat poops, over time the glands' secretions can thicken and harden and the glands become impacted.
• It is important to note changes in the stool that do not relate to other changes, that cannot be accounted for by a change in diet or medication or routine.
• Remember to distinguish between blood on the stool as opposed to blood in the stool.
• To accept the stool's invitation to dance, the bowel's muscles and nerves need to be in good dance form, supplied with adequate levels of needed nutrients.
• A diet lacking appropriate fiber sources for the cat's gut bacteria can lead to constipation.
• Obesity can contribute to constipation.
• Various health conditions and medications can affect bowel action and stool formation.
• Inflammation is the body's initial and innate response to whatever goes wrong, a 911 response to trouble of any kind.
• Large hairballs which manage to go down the wrong way, the long way, can result in an inflamed or impacted small intestine. Even small hairballs can be difficult to inch along.

• One reader administers a small amount of egg yolk lecithin to her cats daily to reduce the incidence of hairballs.
• The musculature of the healthy large intestine is remarkably strong.
• Straining to poop can result in vomiting.
• Any treatment for constipation, including laxatives and enemas, addresses the water retention in the poop and/or the bowel one way or another.

Acute Treatment

• The first thing to do if your cat is suffering an acute bout of constipation is to contact the vet.
• The unique sensitivity of cats as a species means any treatment, whether short or long term, must be especially safe.
• If the accumulated stool in the rectum is too large to pass comfortably through the anus in response to the signal, and is rock hard, even a small enema can be very uncomfortable for the cat unless the stool is first softened.
• Too much liquid injected into the bowel may result in your cat vomiting rather than pooping. Start low and go slow!
• Please note! When using these little enemas, maintain steady pressure on the plunger or especially the bulb when withdrawing the device so that no suction is created. You do not want to exert suction against those tender rectal tissues.
• Only the single ingredient glycerine should be used as a suppository, in a pediatric size.
• Hairball remedies should never be forced into a struggling cat's mouth.
• Do not give a cat liquid mineral oil by mouth.
• Oral stool softeners are not a quick fix, it takes time to rehydrate the stool.

• Both Lactulose and Miralax are dose-to-effect drugs with a normal stool as the goal.
• We see different brand names, different chemical names, different appliances, but how does the bowel 'see' it?
• Learning to physically monitor the status of the constipated cat's situation helps us select the best approach and when it is time to head immediately to the vet for assistance.

Prevention
• Prevention of constipation addresses the retention of water in the poop one way or another.
• The unique sensitivity of cats as a species means any plan, whether short or long term, must be especially safe.
• We want to prevent constipation, not chase it.
• It is not sufficient to see poop in the litter box, we want to support a healthy gut environment.
• Diet is the foundation of health, though not the only factor.
• Cats do not produce salivary amylase but they do produce pancreatic amylase.
• The question is not whether cats can digest carbohydrates, they can. The question is, what are appropriate carbohydrate sources for cats and what ratio is appropriate in their diet.
• The cat's native diet was not just protein and fat; a mouse offers about three percent carbohydrate and the mouse digestive tract contains some plant material.
• If only protein leftovers are available for gut bacteria to ferment, the more pathogenic bacteria benefit at the expense of the beneficial gut bacteria.
• Since cats have low dietary carbohydrate requirements, what to include is more critical for cats than for us omnivorous humans who can safely eat a much wider variety of plant foods in greater quantity.

• Ideally the chosen diet provides adequate and suitable fiber content but some cats may need additional help.
• Changes to the diet or routine of a cat should be made gradually, to allow the cat to adjust and to permit the digestive tract to adapt.
• Food itself is very nutritious.
• Polyethylene glycol is not propylene glycol, more familiarly called antifreeze. Polyethylene glycol is also not ethylene glycol. It is polyethylene glycol. The differences in chemical formulas matter.
• The amount of water needed to normalize the stool in response to an osmotic laxative is the same amount of water by any other method including diet and dietary fiber.

🐾 More To Read

As I explained in the Introduction, I am not a vet. I am an individual with a desire to understand and learn more, and to share what I learn. This is information I wish I had understood when SEM was alive and we were struggling with the constipation common in kidney disease which SEM had. I surely hope it is helpful to you and your cats.

This work is a labor of both love and regret and while I strived to make it as accurate as possible, new research may render some of the information out of date. To illustrate, it was not that long ago that the existence of the enteric nervous system was unrecognized. My intention is to keep this information current but that is not always possible and life is unpredictable. It is the reader's responsibility to confirm what is read.

We have access to an astonishing volume of useful and interesting information. I recommend reading sites and articles that focus on science and research, not testimonials and rants. Too often we get our information from product advertising. No company advertises negative aspects of its products. The foundation of science is objectivity. Yes, even in scientific research and reporting there are collusions and misrepresentation, but that is the exception rather than the rule.

If you are a visual learner, the web offers animated graphics which illustrate some of the concepts discussed here. For example, there are a number of sites which show, rather than tell, how enzymes work. Good search terms are 'enzymes animated graphics' to see the resultant hits. When I did that search, I got 9,320 hits in 0.41 seconds. Even if

"Cats require purity and simplicity." - SEM

most of those hits are off topic, we only need to view a few to understand enzyme action better.

Many sites are devoted to explaining, to the average reader, in clear language, how the digestive tract and digestive system work. Web browsers allow us to search by asking questions, such as, "How does the digestive tract work?" Posing that question to Google resulted in 4,240,000 hits! Certainly many of those will be worthless for the purpose but again, we only need to read a few to gain a better grasp of the subject. Since every cat comes with a digestive tract, anyone who lives with a cat has a vested interest. Of course each of us humans has a digestive tract, too, and the principles are similar. If the material in this book needs augmentation, the web can provide it. Or a local library can do the same.

This site does not cover what happens once digested nutrients cross the gut wall barrier, here our interests were confined to gut issues, but there is a great deal of information available on the metabolic workings of the body, both text and animated graphics. For anyone interested, all of Gray's Anatomy is available online at several sites including Bartleby.com. One can search all entries in the book from Antrum of Highmore to the Zonule of Zinn. If Henry Gray had lived longer than 34 years, had he not succumbed to smallpox which he caught from the nephew he was tending, perhaps he would have discovered the enteric nervous system in his century.

Gut bacteria and fiber, both dietary fiber and/or functional fiber, are subjects of intense scientific research just now. The medical world now realizes the importance of this population of microscopic organisms who reside on and in us all, recognizes that they are not neutral players or mere annoyances and that the advantages of proper care and keeping of these microorganisms are many. Gut bacteria have been on the job since digestive tracts began, they work for fiber, and so far they have not taken up other careers.

New products appear on the market almost daily, probiotics, prebiotics, fiber this, fiber that. *All product advertising is positive!* Before the ink is dry on a preliminary research report, someone is marketing a new OTC product based on that research, whether or not the research has been replicated, whether or not it applies to oral use, whether or not there is any real foundation to the claims for the product. By supplements, I mean products other than the commonly recognized vitamins and minerals. Supplements are not regulated as drugs are other than to outlaw erroneous advertising claims. Advertising copy writers are astonishingly good at skirting the line. They count on our brains to make the connection between cited research and the product since to do otherwise, to state a connection outright, could draw the unwanted attention of the FDA. Our brains are quite good at making these connections. If we read a legitimate research abstract showing positive results for a supplement or herbal mix on the same page as the product description, we assume that the product in our hand will give the same results as the study or the herb monologues, even though this product may not be the same as used in the study, may never have been studied in cats, or in the worst scenario, the container may not contain what it claims.

Wisdom suggests we focus more on educational, veterinary, medical and scientific sites for information, on the web those sites that end in .edu and .org rather than .com.

This book could not have been written without the contributions and cooperation of many, unwittingly or not, and my very tolerant family, and of course without SEM.

My sincere thanks to everyone including you, Dear Reader. Thank you! 🐾

Feline Constipation ❖ Org

http://commons.wikimedia.org/wiki/File:Nasa_blue_marble.jpg

Name	Date	Note

"Cats require purity and simplicity." – SEM

NOTES

Name	Date	Note

Name	Date	Note

"Cats require purity and simplicity." – SEM

NOTES

Name	Date	Note

Printed in Great Britain
by Amazon

10129320R00079